Pos[...]
Rearrar[...]
Wills and Intestacies

Peter White LLM, FTII,
Solicitor

Longman

ISBN 0 85121 229 8

Published by

Longman Professional and Business Communications Division
Longman Group UK Limited
21–27 Lamb's Conduit Street, London WC1N 3NJ

Associated Offices

Australia	Longman Cheshire Pty Ltd, Longman House, Kings Gardens, 91–97 Coventry Street, South Melbourne, Victoria 3205
Hong Kong	Longman Group (Far East) Limited Cornwall House, 18th Floor, Taikoo Trading Estate, Tong Chong Street, Quarry Bay
Malaysia	Longman Malaysia Sdn Bhd No 3 Jalan Kilang A, Off Jalan Penchala, Petaling Jaya, Selangor, Malaysia
Singapore	Longman Singapore Publishers (Pte) Ltd 25 First Lok Yang Road, Singapore 2262
USA	Longman Group (USA) Inc 500 North Dearborn Street, Chicago, Illinois 60610

First published 1982
Second edition 1986
Third edition 1988

A CIP catalogue record for this book is available from the British Library.

Printed and bound in Great Britain by
Biddles Ltd. Guildford and King's Lynn

Preface

Since the last edition of this book on post-mortem tax planning, there have been many important developments, the most important of which was the Budget on 15th March 1988 which increased the inheritance tax nil rate band to £110,000 and slashed top rates of inheritance tax to a single 40% rate. Other developments include the case of *Russell* v *IRC* [1988] STC 195, and the two Finance Acts of 1987. There has also been a consolidation of the Taxes Act which received the Royal Assent on 9th February 1988; income tax references are given with their 1970 Act derivations in brackets. On 1 May 1987, the 50p fixed stamp duty was abolished on most post-death rearrangements if properly certified in accordance with the Stamp Duty (Exempt Instrument) Regulations 1987.

The book deals with the legal aspects of rearrangements, and contains precedents. Some dispositions need rearrangement regardless of tax. For example, Sir Joseph Jekyll, a former Master of the Rolls, gave his estate to pay the national debt — an act which was described by one peer 'as a very foolish one. He might as well have attempted to stop the middle arch of Blackfriar's Bridge with his full bottomed wig'! Fortunately, his relations were able to have the Will set aside on the grounds that he lacked capacity.

Whatever the dispositions by a Will, on intestacy or otherwise, it is often the case that they can be rearranged to greater advantage for the beneficiaries and, perhaps, to mitigate tax. For example, the circumstances in which a Will was made may well have changed substantially when the testator dies. So, on a death, the questions arise: should anything be done, and, if so, what and how? This book provides the answers.

The law is as at 14 April 1988 and includes the Finance Bill 1988 proposals.

Contents

I Introduction

Many testators go to a lot of trouble and expense to leave behind them a Will which sets out exactly what they want to happen to their estate when they die. Others take less trouble, and some, like Vaughan Hawkins (author of *Hawkins on the Construction of Wills*) die intestate. Whatever path is chosen — testacy or intestacy — the dispositions, trusts and powers that arise on death can often be altered in a number of different ways and this book is designed to look at the opportunities and pitfalls in post-death rearrangements.

WHY REARRANGE?

There are many reasons why beneficiaries or trustees should rearrange dispositions of property comprised in an estate on a death and a detailed look at these will be taken in the following chapters. The main reasons for estate rearrangements include:

- To redirect benefits given by Will or on intestacy from one person to another. For example, a surviving spouse who inherits the whole of the estate of a deceased spouse may wish to provide for children and could enter into a written variation to do so. Another example of where a redirection was appropriate is given in the Canadian case of *re Moss* (1977) 77 DLR (3d) 314, in which a Jehovah's Witness died leaving all his estate to the local Jehovah's Witness congregation. Unfortunately, shortly before his death he had been excommunicated for chewing tobacco and the congregation decided that it would be wrong to accept any benefit under his Will.

- To compromise claims under the Inheritance (Provision for Family and Dependants) Act 1975, but if relief for inheritance tax and capital gains tax is required, the redirection must be effected within two years after the death. If later, relief is only given if a 1975 Act order is made, but this can include a consent order.

- To alter the powers of executors, administrators and trustees. This is particularly important where there are continuing trusts after the administration of the estate has been completed. It is possible sometimes to ensure that by a written variation the personal representatives are given extra powers, for example, to invest, insure and distribute capital, but only if those making the variation are between them also absolutely entitled and are creating trusts over what they were given by Will or intestacy.

- To alter beneficial interests; for example, to enlarge a life interest into an absolute interest where those entitled to capital in remainder agree.
- To disclaim a benefit given by Will or intestacy.
- To redirect a joint tenancy interest, or nominated property.
- Where the testator directs or requests a rearrangement; for example, where he gives his property to his personal representatives on discretionary trusts and leaves it to them to distribute the estate. A request (as opposed to a direction) for a rearrangement is known as a precatory trust.
- To resolve a defect in a Will. For example, it may be uncertain on the face of the Will who is to benefit because of an inadequate description, or it may be that there has been a serious typing error. In these circumstances, rather than go to the Court to resolve the problem, a written variation or agreement might be appropriate.
- To save tax. Inevitably this has taken on great significance and many written variations and some disclaimers redirect property simply to save tax, for example, by ensuring that the testator makes full use of the nil and lower rate band of inheritance tax. For deaths following the budget (which increased the nil rate band to £110,000 with a 40% tax on any balance), if there is a surviving spouse then once the deceased's nil rate band has been used, it may not be sensible to incur the 40% inheritance tax charge on the rearrangement, but rather leave it to the surviving spouse to make potentially exempt transfers.

TYPES OF REARRANGEMENT

There are many ways in which the dispositions of an estate can be rearranged, whether the deceased died testate or intestate. Some are given by statute and others derive from the common law. All are dealt with in succeeding chapters. In brief summary they are:

Written variations of the estate by agreement, which sometimes require Court consent. A class of such variations is deeds of family arrangement, but tax effective written variations are not restricted to these alone. Written variations are dealt with in Chapter II.

Disclaimers Instead of a variation, a disclaimer of an interest may be appropriate, and if the desired result can be produced by a disclaimer it may be better to disclaim rather than to enter into a written variation. Disclaimers are dealt with in Chapter III.

Discretionary Wills Increasingly frequently, a testator will leave his estate or a nil rate band legacy to his executors or trustees on trust for them to distribute as they think fit in their absolute discretion, there will usually be a requirement that the discretion is to be exercised within 23 months after the death, and a provision for gifts over in default of the exercise of the trustees' discretion. These Wills are the ultimate in flexibility and are dealt with in Chapter IV.

Precatory trusts Instead of using a binding discretionary trust, a testator can make a gift of property to a beneficiary coupled with a request (which is not legally binding) that the beneficiary should distribute the property in a particular way — usually in accordance with instructions given in writing before the testator dies. The idea is to keep the distribution of the property as flexible as possible, enabling the testator to change his mind without going through the formality of a new testamentary provision or risking discretionary trusts. Precatory trusts are dealt with in Chapter V.

Lifetime Gifts There is nothing to stop a person making a simple gift of a benefit given to him by Will or intestacy. Whether a gift is a potentially exempt or chargeable transfer itself, or qualifies for relief under the post-death variation rules depends on how it is worded. The Revenue practice, however, requires reference to variation — see page 12.

Capitalisation of life interest on intestacy A surviving spouse has the statutory right to capitalise the statutory life interest given her on intestacy, taking a capital sum in lieu of the right to income. This is dealt with in Chapter V.

Family Provision orders Orders in favour of the deceased's family and dependants under the Inheritance (Provision for Family and Dependants) Act 1975 constitute estate rearrangements and are dealt with in Chapter VI.

INHERITANCE TAX

Inheritance tax was introduced by FA 1986 for transfers of value made, and other events occurring, on or after 18 March 1986. Rearrangements made after 17 March 1986 in respect of deaths before then, if effective, will have been within the capital transfer tax regime; rearrangements in respect of deaths from then on are within the inheritance tax regime. So when an election is made, the appropriate statutory reference in the election is that applicable at the date of the death.

The inheritance tax provisions of FA 1986 amending the 1984 Act, had little direct effect on the post-death rearrangements legislation. The only specific change is in IHTA 1984, s 142(5) that property comprised in a person's estate does not include property to which he is treated as entitled by virtue of the reservation of benefit rules in FA 1986, s 102. Such property does not actually form part of the deceased's estate and must have been subject to an earlier lifetime gift, so it is not unreasonable that the donee should not be able to take the opportunity of the deceased donor's death to pass on the gifted property to another without inheritance tax. F(No 2)A 1987 gave relief on post-death rearrangements from certain anti-avoidance provisions when the potentially exempt transfer regime was extended to invest in possession trusts (see p 43).

Like capital transfer tax, inheritance tax is levied on lifetime gifts and on death except that transfers of value which are made by an individual on or after 18 March 1986 and which would otherwise be chargeable transfers, are potentially exempt transfers to the extent that they constitute either a gift to an individual or into an accumulation and maintenance trust or a disabled trust. For lifetime transfers made after 16th March 1987, gifts interest in possession trusts are also potentialy exempt transfers, and transfers out of such trusts qualify to the extent that a beneficiary acquires an absolute interest, or an interest in possession, or an accumulation and maintenance trust is created. A potentially exempt transfer is only chargeable if the donor dies within seven years, and tapering relief is given after three years. Relevant tables are set out in the back of this book. So if an individual makes a potentially exempt transfer and survives seven years without reservation of benefit, the gift is not chargeable and drops out of account because the cumulation period is by FA 1986 seven years.

The possibility of making potentially exempt transfers is an important consideration in deciding on post-death rearrangements. A surviving spouse, for example, may decide to keep the bulk of what she is given by her deceased husband and pass it on by lifetime gifts, rather than vary the dispositions of her husband's estate. However, the advantages of a tax-effective variation of over a lifetime gift include the following:

- A variation will be treated as a gift by the deceased, whereas a gift could be chargeable on a death within seven years.
- The reservation of benefit rules do not apply to tax-effective variations and disclaimers whereas they can apply to gifts.
- In any event, it is almost always sensible to use up the deceased's nil rate band where property passes to an exempt beneficiary.

- The ability to make potentially exempt transfers is almost certain to be withdrawn on a change of Government and by then it may be too late to make a tax-effective variation.

The guide lines for deciding whether or not to make the election on a written variation within two years after a death are on page 16.

The reservation of benefit rules

FA 1986 introduces reservation of benefit rules which are contained in s 102. This applies where, on or after 18 March 1986, an individual disposes of any property by way of lifetime gift and either:

(a) possession and enjoyment of the property is not *bona fide* assumed by the donee at or before the beginning of the relevant period; or
(b) at any time in the relevant period the property is not enjoyed to the entire exclusion, or virtually the entire exclusion, of the donor and of any benefit to him by contract or otherwise.

The 'relevant period' means the period ending on the date of the donor's death and beginning seven years before that date, or if it is later, on the date of the gift.

Property subject to such a reservation is treated as being part of the donor's estate on death for the purpose of the 1984 Act or, if the reservation ends before death, the donor is treated for the purpose of the 1984 Act as making a potentially exempt transfer at the time the reservation is released.

The reservation of benefit rules do not apply, inter alia, to transfers which qualify for the following exemptions:

(1) the spouse exemption;
(2) the small gifts exemption;
(3) gifts in consideration of marriage;
(4) gifts to charity;
(5) gifts to political parties;
(6) gifts for national purposes, etc;
(7) gifts for the public benefit;
(8) maintenance funds for historic buildings; and
(9) employee trusts.

The rules will apply, for example, if the settlor of a discretionary trust is a beneficiary: *Gartside* v *IRC* [1968] AC 553; if the donor occupies a house which he has given away; and if the settlor can charge remuneration as a trustee of the settlement he created: *Oakes* v *Commissioner of Stamp Duty* [1954] AC 57. A reservation of benefit must be distinguished from a retention of an interest: *Commissioner of Stamp Duty* v *Perpetual Trustee Company* [1943]

AC 425, and *Munro* v *Commissioner of Stamp Duty* [1934] AC 61. So, for example, a donor can settle property on another for life and keep the reversionary interest. All the donor is giving away is the life interest and no benefit is reserved from that. A donor can also be the trustee of the settlement which he or she creates: *Oakes (Supra)*.

Although these rules apply to lifetime gifts, including potentially exempt transfers, they do not apply to variation or disclaimers, nor to precatory trusts.

One final point. If the donor under a written variation does specifically reserve a benefit, that benefit could negate the effect of the relieving provisions in s 142 because they do not apply to a variation or disclaimer made for any consideration in money or money's worth other than consideration consisting of the making, in respect of another of the dispositions, of a variation or disclaimer to which s 142 applies. This is relevant, for example, if a variation is made in favour of a beneficiary who pays the person making the variation an annuity in return for it.

NATURE OF A BENEFICIARY'S INTEREST IN AN ESTATE

The effect of many rearrangements depends to some extent on the beneficiary's interest in the assets affected by the arrangement. It is therefore important to appreciate the nature of that beneficiary's interest in the deceased's estate.

On death, assets of the deceased passing by Will or intestacy (but not those passing by survivorship or nomination) vest in the deceased's personal representatives who are entitled to the legal estate in the assets, but the beneficiaries are not necessarily entitled to a beneficial interest until completion of administration. This can, and does, cause difficulty, and bearing in mind that those who are given pecuniary legacies have no interest in the estate assets themselves, the rules are:

Specific gifts

It appears that the beneficiary of a specific gift has a beneficial interest in the property subject to the personal representatives' right to resort to it for the payment of debts. In *IRC* v *Hawley* (1927) 13 TC 327, however, it was held that dividends arising in respect of a specific gift before assent nevertheless formed part of the income of the beneficiary, but only retrospectively as a result of an assent to the vesting of shares in the beneficiary. The implications of this can be important for income tax.

Residuary gifts

The nature of a residuary beneficiary's entitlement depends on whether administration of the estate has been completed. There is no general rule as to when administration ends, and it depends on the facts in relation to any particular asset, but at the latest it will be when the personal representatives assent to a beneficiary (which must be in writing, in the case of land) or, if earlier, when residue is ascertained. Residue will be ascertained when the amount due to residuary beneficiaries is known, and this will usually be when the final estate accounts have been drawn up and all liabilities settled or provided for.

Administration not completed

Until administration ends, the whole of the legal and equitable interest in residue is vested in the personal representatives (or, before a grant of administration, in the President of the Family Division) and the only right of a beneficiary is to require the estate to be duly administered: *Commissioners of Stamp Duties (Queensland)* v *Livingston* [1965] AC 694. This right can be enforced through the Courts by an administration action, and is one that has value for inheritance tax purposes. It is also, apparently, an asset for capital gains tax, being a *chose in action*. The lack of a beneficial interest can cause problems, however. It has served to deprive a beneficiary of a full right to compensation on a compulsory acquisition (*Eastbourne Mutual Building Society* v *Hastings Corporation* [1965] 1 All ER 779), and has deprived a beneficiary who was given property of the right to resist a possession action (*Lall* v *Lall* [1965] 3 All ER 330). It can also cause difficulties with *post mortem* rearrangements and capital gains tax.

Administration completed

As soon as administration has been completed, even though the personal representatives continue to hold estate assets, the beneficiary becomes entitled to a beneficial (or legal interest) in the relevant assets and the personal representatives hold the assets on trust for the beneficiary.

II Written variations

WHO CAN VARY?

Adults
A variation of the dispositions of a Will or on intestacy can be made by anyone whose interest is affected by the variation, so long as they are of full age and capacity and absolutely entitled to the interest concerned. Such a beneficiary can by variation make an outright gift of his or her interest to another, or settle it for the benefit of others.

Example
A inherits £200,000 under B's Will. A wishes to provide for his children and so executes a Deed of Variation of B's Will under which A's children take between them £25,000, contingent on reaching the age of 25. A is left with £175,000.

A variation by beneficiaries can also be effective where trusts or trust interests are created on death, either:

- by a disposition of that trust interest; or
- by bringing the trust to an end; or
- by giving the trustees greater dispositive or administrative powers.

In the latter two cases, the termination or variation is effective under the rule in *Saunders* v *Vautier* (1841) 4 Beav 115 which permits beneficiaries who are *sui juris* and together entitled to the whole beneficial interest to put an end to the trusts and require the trustees to hand over property, as they direct. This rule does not, however, enable such beneficiaries to control the exercise of the trustees' discretions, if they decide to allow the trusts to continue: *Morley* v *Moore* [1936] 2 KB 359.

Example
C's Will gives property to D for life remainder to E and both are *sui juris*. Possible variations include:

(1) D gives his life interest to another, including, if he wishes, E; or
(2) D disclaims it, as to which see Chapter III; or
(3) E gives his interest in remainder to another; or
(4) E disclaims his interest; or

(5) D and E agree to terminate the trusts and divide the capital between them;
(6) D and E agree to keep the trusts going but can give the trustees wider power of investment.

Absolute gifts to surviving spouse
The simplest, most flexible disposition by Will is for each spouse to leave everything to the other. On the death of the first the survivor has three choices: first, to keep all or part of the inherited property; secondly, within two years to enter into a post-death rearrangement to pass on property to others; and thirdly, to make lifetime potentially exempt transfers which drop out of account after seven years if the donor reserves no benefit. There are problems with absolute gifts like this: the surviving spouse may decide to take no action even though it would be sensible fiscally and financially to do so. Another important problem is that a post-death rearrangement and a lifetime gift by the surviving spouse could be caught by the income tax anti-avoidance provisions, particularly if made in favour of minor children when distributed income is treated as that of the surviving spouse and not that of the children (see p 26).

Those incapable of giving consent
Where beneficiaries are incapable of giving their consent to a variation, for example, because they are minors, mentally incapable or simply unborn or unascertained, consent can be given on their behalf by the Court. This is usually given under the Variation of Trusts Act 1958, although the Court does have a power to effect compromises and arrangements on behalf of minors and unascertained beneficiaries under Trustee Act 1925, s 57.

The Variation of Trusts Act 1958 gives the Court very wide jurisdiction to approve all sorts of variations, including variations of beneficial interests, on behalf of:

(1) any person having, directly or indirectly, an interest, whether vested or contingent, under the trusts, who by reason of infancy or other incapacity is incapable of assenting; or
(2) any person (whether ascertained or not) who may become entitled, directly or indirectly, to an interest under the trusts as being at a future date or on the happening of a future event ('future' here meaning any time after the date of application to the Court) a person of any specified description or a member of any specified class of persons; or
(3) any person unborn; or
(4) any person in respect of their discretionary interest under protective trusts where the interest of the principal beneficiary has not failed or determined.

The Court has no power to give consent on behalf of someone who is capable of doing so but who declines to do so.

Court approval will only be given if the arrangement is for the benefit of the person or persons on behalf of whom consent is being given (except those listed in (4) above, whom an arrangement does not have to benefit).

Example
F's Will gives property to G for life with remainder to such of G's descendants as are living at G's death. A variation is proposed whereby the trust property is to be divided between G and his three adult children, with provisions being made for any minor children or grandchildren and (by way of insurance policy, perhaps) unborn descendants. The Court would have to approve this under the Variation of Trusts Act 1958 on behalf of both minor and unborn beneficiaries.

The problems with obtaining Court consent
There are a number of obvious problems with obtaining Court consent which make it undesirable to have to seek it. They are:

- it is expensive, so the tax saving involved must be substantial to make proceedings worthwhile; and
- it takes time and this can cause problems with the two year time limit; and
- the variation will not be approved by the Court unless it is for the benefit of those in respect of whom the Court consent is given.

Possible solutions
There are two main ways of resolving the problem of obtaining Court consent. The first is to have a discretionary legacy or Will (see Chapter IV). The second is that it is thought possible that specific provision can be made in the Will to the effect that parents or guardians of beneficiaries who are incapable, or trustees for those unascertained, can give consent on behalf of those who cannot themselves consent. Care must be taken when conferring this power to ensure that its mere existence does not defeat accumulation and maintenance trusts in a Will, and it is sensible to impose suitable restrictions on the exercise of the power to the extent that such trusts would otherwise subsist.

INHERITANCE TAX

The relief
When testamentary dispositions are varied, someone will inevitably benefit at the expense of another, so that the estate of the latter will diminish with possible inheritance tax consequences. To avoid a

second potential charge to inheritance tax when this happens IHTA 1984, s 142(1) provides that where within two years after a person's death any of the dispositions (whether effected by Will, under the law relating to intestacy or otherwise) of the property comprised in his estate immediately before his death are varied by a written instrument made by the persons or any of the persons who benefit or would benefit under the dispositions, the Act shall apply as if the variation had been effected by the deceased. Section 17(a) also provides that the variation itself is not a transfer of value and it cannot therefore be either a potentially exempt transfer or chargeable.

For s 142 and s 17(a) to apply, an election must, by s 142(2), be given by written notice to the Board of Inland Revenue within six months after the variation (or such longer time as the Board may allow) by the persons making it and, if the variation results in more tax being payable, by the personal representatives. Personal representatives may decline to join in an election only if no, or no sufficient, assets are held by them in that capacity for discharging the additional tax. So where the personal representative is required to join in the election the position is that if they hold as personal representative sufficient assets to pay the additional tax, they must join in the election: if they are not sufficiently funded, they may decline the join in the election and s 142(1) will not apply. Should this problem exist, the solution is either to fund the personal representatives or to give them sufficient indemnities.

The election can be included in the variation itself and should be sent to the Capital Taxes Office, Minford House, Rockley Road, London W1H 0DF, and to the Inspector of Taxes if the capital gains tax election is made.

Example

H dies having made no lifetime chargeable transfers in the seven years before his death. He leaves his £300,000 estate as to one half to his wife, I, and as to the other half to his two adult children, J and K. The £150,000 going to J and K is therefore chargeable and the inheritance tax bill is £16,000.

If, however, J decided to give his mother another £15,000, a lifetime gift would be a potentially exempt transfer and would have to be taken into account if J died within seven years, but would in any event presumably be within J's nil rate band.

If, on the other hand, the £15,000 were to be given to I within two years after H's death under a written variation within IHTA 1984, s 142, then provided that an election is made within six months thereafter, the gift by J is not a transfer of value by J, and H is treated as giving £165,000 to I by Will. H's chargeable estate is therefore reduced to

£135,000 and the inheritance tax bill reduced to £10,000, a saving of £6,000.

Revenue Practice
Some doubt at one time existed about Revenue practice on written variations and in 1985 they issued a statement which was published in the Law Society's Gazette on 22 May 1985 at page 1454 and is printed at [1985] STI 298. This requires the following conditions to be satisfied by an instrument if it is to be brought within s 142:

(1) The instrument in writing must be made by the persons or any of the persons who benefit or would benefit under the dispositions of the property comprised in the deceased's estate immediately before his death.
(2) The instrument must be made within two years after the death.
(3) The instrument must clearly indicate the dispositions that are the subject of it, and vary their destination as laid down by the deceased's Will, or under the law relating to intestate estates, or otherwise.
(4) A notice of election must be given within six months of the date of the instrument, unless the Board see fit to accept a late election.
(5) The notice of election must refer to the appropriate statutory provision.

The statement also states: "It will not be contended that the instrument of variation, to be eligible, has in terms to be purport to vary the Will or intestacy provisions themselves: it is sufficient that the instrument of variation identifies the disposition to be varied and buries its destination. It is emphasised, however, that the Revenue will continue to require that the provisions of s 142 as interpreted above, are satisfied."

Deeds of family arrangement
The relief given by s 142 is not in any way restricted simply to deeds of family arrangement, although before FA 1978 it was limited to deeds of family arrangement or similar instruments. So, although deeds of family arrangement are, as variations, within the scope of the inheritance tax relief, there is now no need for a variation to be a deed of family arrangement or similar instrument. As a matter of interest, deed of family arrangement is:

> "an agreement between members of the same family, intended to be generally and reasonably for the benefit of the family either by compromising doubtful or disputed rights or by preserving the family property or the peace and security of the family by avoiding litigation or by saving its honour."

Consideration
The relief does not apply to a variation made for any consideration in money or money's worth other than consideration consisting of the making in respect of another of the dispositions, of a variation or disclaimer to which s 142(1) applies: s 142(3).

This applies to any form of consideration, but the purpose of s 142(3) seems to be to prevent the misuse of the spouse exemption whereby a chargeable beneficiary might agree to vary the dispositions of an estate so that a surviving spouse takes instead, but pays him out of her own resources. Such an arrangement does not qualify for relief.

Similarly, if a beneficiary who was given a residence by the deceased, varies the deceased's dispositions in favour of his children in consideration of his children permitting him to reside there for a period of time, s 142 would not apply and to the extent that the variation constituted a gift then the right to remain in residence could amount to a benefit reserved: see *Nichols* v *IRC* [1975] STC 278, and, in any event, his occupation could amount to an interest in possession if his right to occupy was for life. On the other hand, if the beneficiary varied the dispositions so that he was given a lease and the reversion was given to his children, s 142 could apply.

It appears that if a beneficiary varies a disposition to transfer property which is subject to a liability, the recipient's agreement to take on that liability is outside the scope of s 142(3).

Reservation of benefit
The effect of making a valid election in respect of a post-death written variation or of making a disclaimer within two years after death is, by s 142(1), that the 1984 Act shall apply as if the variation had been effected by the deceased or, as the case may be, the disclaimed benefit never conferred, and by IHTA 1984, s 17(*a*) the variation or disclaimer is not a transfer of value. Thus the deceased is to be treated as making the variation and is therefore to be regarded as the donor of any gift effected by the variation. Any benefit reserved to the person actually making the variation or disclaimer cannot be within the scope of the reservation of benefit rules in s 102. It is true that FA 1986, s 102 is not part of the 1984 Act and *prima facie* the relieving provisions do not apply because they only relate to the provisions of the 1984 Act. However, the charging provisions in s 102(3) and (4) above apply 'for the purposes of the 1984 Act' which must include the provisions in s 142, and, in any event, the inheritance tax provisions of FA 1986 are to be construed as one with the 1984 Act: FA 1986, s 114(5).

The consequence is that, for example, a beneficiary of a house under a Will can vary the deceased's dispositions so that the house passes to children but the beneficiary can continue to remain in residence without s 102 applying subject to the point on consideration above. Also, a legatee of an absolute gift by Will can create discretionary trusts over that gift under which the legatee is a discretionary beneficiary, and if a valid s 142 election is made, there will be no scope for s 102 to apply.

Dead beneficiaries

The inheritance tax and capital gains tax rules apply even though a beneficiary is dead, and the variation is made by his personal representatives. Such a variation can be made to reduce the estate of a deceased beneficiary and the Revenue also accept that the variation can be made to increase the estate despite authority that a deed cannot increase the value of an estate of someone already dead: re *Corbisley's Trusts* (1880) 14 Ch. D 846; re *Tilt, Lampeter* v *Kennedy* (1896) LT 163.

> *Example*
>
> L dies leaving all his property to his children. His widow, M, dies shortly thereafter. The children could vary the dispositions of L's estate so that all or some of it passes into M's estate, to take advantage of the spouse exemption. The property passing into M's estate would then devolve under M's dispositions and at M's inheritance tax rates.
>
> If, on the other hand, the estate had been left entirely to M and she died prematurely having survived her husband, her personal representatives could arrange to vary her husband's estate, for example, to give sufficient to the children, to effect a form of equalisation of estates for the two of them and thus minimising tax.

If on such a variation the ultimate destination of the property in each estate is the same as it would have been under the two Wills, the principle in *IRC* v *Ramsay* [1981] STC 174 as extended and explained in *Furniss* v *Dawson* [1984] STC 153 TCA 621, needs to be considered. Where there is a preordained series of transactions or a single 'composite' transaction which may or may not include the achievement of a legitimate commercial purpose; and a step or steps are inserted which have no commercial or business purpose (as opposed to effect) other than the avoidance of liability to tax, then the court must look at the end result and disregard a step or steps inserted for fiscal purposes. It is thought, however, that this principle does not apply since dispositions on death and gifts are not 'transactions'.

The estate

Section 142 only applies to a variation of the dispositions of the property comprised in the deceased's estate. This includes excluded property but does not include trust property in which the deceased had an interest in possession and which he is therefore treated as owning by s 49(1): s 142(5), but see p 43 for relief where the life interest is followed by discretionary trusts, or the life tenant has wide powers of appointment. This exclusion of trust property is not unreasonable, since it will almost certainly pass to a third person by virtue of the trust instrument and the deceased would have no control over it. It is conceivable, however, that the deceased could own an interest on the life of another which passes on his death.

The estate of a deceased person does not include property which the deceased is treated as owning because it was subject to the reservation of benefit rules in s 102: s 142(5). Since such property has already been given away by the deceased during his lifetime and therefore does not actually form part of his estate, it is not unreasonable that the s 142 rules should not apply.

A deceased's estate does include, however, property passing by his Will, by the law relating to intestacy or otherwise, so that a joint tenancy interest and nominated property are within the scope of the s 142 rules.

Increases in value

Any variation takes effect in relation to property comprised in the deceased's estate at the date of his death, and if that property subsequently increases in value, it should be possible to pass on the increase in value without inheritance tax, or for the original beneficiary to keep the increase in value but to pass on the gifted property itself.

Example

L dies leaving his £200,000 estate to his wife M absolutely. Within two years of his death, the value of the estate increases to £350,000. M wishes to keep the £200,000 but is prepared to give away the £150,000 increase to the children.

She can do this within two years of L's death by rearranging the dispositions of his Will so that the Will provides that she is given a legacy of £200,000 with residue to go to children. Since the estate value at the date of death is only £200,000, the whole of this is attributed to her legacy (IHTA 1984, s 38) and the children take the balance free of inheritance tax.

If the £200,000 had been given by L's Will to his children instead, and if they had wished to provide for their mother, the children (if of full age) could enter into a variation of the Will by which their mother could take a legacy of £200,000 and residue would pass to them. The whole of the estate would again be free of inheritance tax because it now passes to an exempt beneficiary and the children would take the increase in value tax free. It would be even more tax efficient if the children were to take the amount of L's nil rate band also.

Whether to make the election

As described on p 11, the election must be made by written notice given to the Board of Inland Revenue within six months after the date of the instrument, or such longer time as the Board may allow. It is thought that there have to be exceptional circumstances for late notice to be accepted and inadvertence is not sufficient excuse.

It is important to consider whether or not the s 142(2) election should be made, and in some cases it may be better not to.

Example

N dies in April 1988 having made £110,000 worth of lifetime chargeable transfers (including potentially exempt transfers) within the seven years before his death. He leaves his estate as to one half to his wife O and as to the other half in equal shares to his two children P and Q. All are adults. The value of his estate is £200,000, so £100,000 goes to the children and is chargeable to inheritance tax of £40,000. There are three possible types of variation which could be made within two years after N's death:

Variation A

P and Q give up property worth £50,000 to O. If an election is made, the chargeable estate on N's death will be reduced to £50,000 and the inheritance tax bill reduced to £20,000. If no election is made, the inheritance tax on the estate will be unchanged and each of P and Q will on the variation be making a gift to their mother of £25,000 which will be a potentially exempt transfer and (subject to the annual exemption) chargeable only if either dies within seven years and then, because the charge is retrospective to the gift, the nil rate band and exemptions should be sufficient to cover it.

Variation B

On the other hand, if P were to give up property worth £50,000 to Q and an election is made, N's chargeable estate will be unchanged and inheritance tax will be the same. If no election is made, the variation will mean that P will, in addition, be treated as making a gift of £50,000.

Variation C

If O were to give up property worth £50,000 to her two children, the chargeable estate on N's death will be increased to £150,000 and the inheritance tax bill will be increased to £60,000, should an election be made. If no election is made, the inheritance tax on N's death will be unaffected and at the date of the variation O will be treated as making a gift of £50,000 to her children. This gift is a potentially exempt transfer (subject to the annual exemption) and is chargeable only if she dies within seven years without reservation of benefit.

Conclusion
Whether an election should be made depends on all the circumstances. If the person making the variation intends to reserve a benefit within the scope of FA 1986, s 102, then serious consideration should be given to making the election so that the reservation of benefit rules do not apply. It will usually be sensible to make an election where the amount of inheritance tax is reduced as a result of the variation, in other words where the person who benefits from the variation is an exempt beneficiary. On the other hand, if an exempt beneficiary is losing as a result of the variation, an election will generally not be desirable if it increases the overall tax bill but it could still be sensible, for example to use up the deceased's nil rate band, or to avoid an increase in the estate of an already rich beneficiary although since 16 March 1988 it has become less fiscally undesirable to increase the estates of the rich. Where chargeable beneficiaries are giving up assets to other chargeable beneficiaries by the variation, an election is almost always sensible, but will not be sensible, for example, where one chargeable beneficiary is married to the beneficiary of the variation so that the variation itself is within the scope of the spouse exemption.

Grossing up pitfall
Where an estate is partly chargeable, partly exempt, IHTA 1984, ss 36–42 require the grossing up of chargeable gifts which do not bear their own tax. By IHTA 1984, s 211, the rule is that inheritance tax on all gifts is a testamentary expense and thus payable primarily out of residue, like any other unsecured debt, so that, as a general rule, chargeable legacies will not bear their own inheritance tax.

If a written variation is treated as being made by the deceased, it will be subject where relevant to ss 36–42 and problems can arise. Here is an extreme example:

Example
R died in June 1987 leaving an estate worth £40,000 which he left to his wife S. He had made chargeable gifts of £257,000 in the last seven years before his death so the relevant tax rate on the estate is 50%. S decides that she would like their son T to receive half the estate, so she executes a written variation whereby R's Will is to be read as if T took a legacy of £20,000. No reference is made to the inheritance tax burden.

> If the election is made to treat the variation as having been effected by the deceased, then because the legacy is implicitly free of inheritance it must be grossed up at the relevant death rate (here 50%) and the grossed-up value of £20,000 at 50% is £40,000. The distribution of the estate would be £20,000 to T, £20,000 to the Inland Revenue and nothing to S. If the burden of inheritance tax is imposed on T's £20,000 legacy by the variation, the distribution will be £10,000 to T, £10,000 to the Inland Revenue and £20,000 to S.

The same principle applies with a top rate of 40%.

Using grossing up

It used to be possible to use the grossing up provisions to advantage where the estate included assets qualifying for business property relief or agricultural relief if there was an exempt beneficiary, because s 38(1) provides that such part of the value transferred shall be attributable to specific gifts as corresponds to the value of the gifts. So the fact that the *value transferred* (as reduced) had to be apportioned to the *value* of the gifts gave rise to avoidance possibilities. This was one of the points in *Russell* v *IRC* [1988] STC 195 which is dealt with on page 21 below. It was held that such arrangements could be effective but only to the extent either that the specific gifts to chargeable beneficiaries were of business assets *in specie* or they were pecuniary legacies which could only be satisfied out of business assets.

However, FA 1986, s 105 introduced new provisions which apply in respect to transfers of value made on or after 18 March 1986. Section 105 introduced a new s 39A into the IHTA 1984 and this provides that where any part of the value transferred by a transfer of value is attributable to the value of relevant business property or to the agricultural value of agricultural property then:

(a) specific gifts (pecuniary and specific legacies) of such property are to be treated as being of their reduced value, and
(b) other specific gifts are to be taken as the 'appropriate fraction' of their values. The numerator of this fraction is the value transferred less the reduced value of the gifts in (a), and the denominator is the value before the relevant relief of the transfer of value less the unreduced value of the gifts in (a).

The idea is to apportion the business property relief to gifts (other than specific gifts of qualifying property) and residue.

> *Example*
>
> U dies and leaves a legacy of £200,000 to his son subject to inheritance tax and the residue of his estate worth £100,000 to his wife. His estate includes £200,000 worth of a controlling interest in

shares in his trading company. The value transferred of the shares after business property relief of 50% is £100,000 and so the value transferred on death is a total of £200,000 and not the £300,000 actual value.

For deaths before 18 March 1986 the whole of the £200,000 value transferred could be attributed as a gift to the son (see *Russell* above) and that was fully chargeable.

It was then open to the son and the surviving spouse to enter into a variation whereby the surviving spouse was given a legacy of £100,000 and the son would be given residue, worth £200,000. The s 38 rules required that the first £100,000 worth of the value transferred be attributed to the wife's legacy and the balance of the value transferred — £100,000 — to residue so that £100,000 only would be chargeable but the same distribution of the estate would be achieved.

As a result of FA 1986, business property relief is apportioned *pro rata* between the legacy to the son and residue to the widow so under the original dispositions by the Will, the apportionment would be (see (b) above):

$$\frac{200{,}000 - \text{nil}}{300{,}000 - \text{nil}} \times 200{,}000 = £133{,}333$$

If the variation is made, the amount apportioned to the specific legacy of £100,000 to the spouse will be:

$$\frac{100{,}000 - \text{nil}}{300{,}000 - \text{nil}} \times 100{,}000 = £\ 33{,}333$$

and the balance (£166,667) will be the chargeable gift to the son.

Gifts

The second part of s 142(6) suggests that a beneficiary can make an inheritance tax effective variation by way of gift. It states that s 142(1) applies whether or not the administration of the estate is complete or the property concerned has been distributed in accordance with the original dispositions. This means that a beneficiary can simply make a gift of property, or of an interest derived from a Will or intestacy, once he has received it, provided that all the other requirements of s 142 are satisfied, including the requirement that the election must also be made by the personal representatives where the gift results in additional tax being payable. However, in view of the Revenue practice (see page 12, above) it would be foolhardy to attempt a s 142 election without complying with all their requirements, including that which requires the document to vary the destination of the dispositions. On the other hand, a lifetime gift which is a potentially exempt transfer, may be intended, and there is no question of an election.

Short interests created by the variation
Section 142(4) provides that where a variation to which s 142(1) applies results in property being held in trust for a person for a period which ends not more than two years after the death, inheritance tax is levied as if the disposition of the property at the end of that period had had effect from the beginning of the period. This means that such short term interests will be ignored, but whether the ultimate beneficiary is treated as receiving the property as at the date of death depends on whether a s 142(2) election was made in respect of the variation itself. It appears that s 142(4) does not apply to ignore a life interest created by a variation which comes to an end within the two year period on the death of the life tenant, because s 142(4) requires that the variation itself must *result* in the property being held for the short term, and not a termination from natural causes.

Multiple variations
The effect of s 142 on multiple variations is, at first sight, unclear. For example, could a residuary beneficiary execute three separate variations each in respect of a one third share of residue in favour of different beneficiaries, or in favour of the same beneficiary? The latter type of arrangement was popular when stamp duty was leviable, in order to keep each gift within the £30,000 *ad valorem* stamp duty limit. Also it was not clear whether a beneficiary under a variation could then vary the varied dispositions of the deceased's estate to redirect the benefit received.

The Revenue Statement in [1985] STI 298 states:

> 'There have been some cases in which a number of instruments of variation have been executed in relation to the same Will or intestacy. The Revenue emphasise that these cases must be considered on their precise facts, but in broad terms their view will be as follows:
>
> (a) an election which is validly made is irrevocable;
> (b) an instrument will not fall within CTTA 1984, s 142 if it *further* redirects any item or any part of an item that has *already* been redirected under an earlier instrument;
> (c) to avoid any uncertainty, variations covering a number of items should ideally be made in one instrument'.

The effectiveness of a second variation of the same property comprised in an estate was considered in *Russell* v *IRC* [1988] STC 195. A testator died in 1983 survived by his wife and four daughters. His estate included Lloyds underwriting assets which qualified for

50% business property relief and he left the bulk of it to his widow, so it was exempt. To take advantage of business property relief and his unused nil rate band, the widow executed a Deed of Variation giving each of her four daughters a pecuniary legacy of £25,000. The nil rate band at the time was £55,000 and the idea was that the value of the gifts for inheritance tax would (as a result of s 38 dealt with on page 18 above) be £50,000 and not the true value of £100,000. The Revenue refused to accept this proposition and the widow and the daughters with the executors entered into a second variation in 1985, still within the two year period, giving each daughter a share of the business assets worth £25,000. The Revenue accepted that the 1985 Deed qualified for businesss property relief but did not accept that it was within what is now s 142. Knox J held that it was impossible to import into s 142, relief for a second variation of the same property. That would in effect be to make s 142 apply to dispositions under s 142. Such a tortuous process would merit a specific reference in the enactment itself. Once Parliament had swallowed the camel of allowing testamentary dispositions to be rewritten, no compelling reason existed as to why it should strain at the gnat of allowing a second attempt.

Foreign element

Excluded property is within the scope of s 142. Property situated overseas is excluded property if the person beneficially entitled to it is an individual domiciled outside the UK: IHTA 1984, s 6. Also, property comprised in a settlement situated outside the UK is excluded property unless the settlor was UK domiciled at the time the settlement was made: s 48.

These rules can be used to advantage. For example, if the deceased is not UK domiciled, a UK beneficiary could vary the deceased's dispositions to create either an interest in possession settlement or discretionary trust of which he is one of the beneficiaries. The settlement will then be treated as having been made by the deceased and so long as the property remains situated overseas, it is excluded property even though the beneficiaries are UK domiciled. Further, the reservation of benefit rules will not apply.

However, there are income tax problems. The person making the variation is the settlor for income tax and to the extent that that person does not become entitled to income, an income tax liability could arise under TA 1988, s 739 (s 478) (Transfer of Assets Abroad) if the beneficiary has 'power to enjoy' the income; or if the beneficiary retains an interest or is the object of a discretionary power, s 673 (s 447) and s 674 (s 448) apply. S 673 (s 447) catches accumulated income where the settlor or spouse retains an interest in income or capital (except in certain specified cases, such as in the event of the death under the age of 25 of a person who would be beneficially entitled to income or capital on attaining that age). S 674 (s 448) catches all income of a settlement where there is a power to pay or apply income or property to the benefit of a trustee or spouse. In both cases, the income is taxed as that of the settlor for all income tax purposes.

There may be a capital gains tax problem, too. S 49(6) (see below) applies to s 49 only and not to the capital gains tax legislation as a whole. The consequence is that the settlement may be treated as having been made by the beneficiary for other capital gains tax purposes, for example the remittance basis in FA 1981, s 80.

CAPITAL GAINS TAX

Similar provisions to those which apply to inheritance tax exist for capital gains tax in CGTA 1979, s 49(6)–(9).Despite the Budget provisions eliminating pre-March 1982 gains, capital gains tax remains a substantial problem, particularly as gains are now treated as a top slice of income.

By s 49(6), where within the period of two years after a person's death any of the dispositions (whether effected by Will, under the law relating to intestacy or otherwise) of the property of which he was competent to dispose are varied, by an instrument in writing made by the persons or any of the persons who benefit or would benefit under the dispositions, the variation is not a disposal and s 49 applies as if it had been effected by the deceased provided that an election to this effect is made within six months after the variation. The consequence is that when the beneficiary of the variation takes the property, he takes as legatee under the Will and thus is treated as acquiring the property from the personal representatives at market value at the date of the death by virtue of s 49(4). The result is to eliminate the disposal which would otherwise have been made on the variation, thus postponing the realisation of any inherent gain or loss.

The provisions only apply to property of which the deceased was competent to dispose. This is defined by s 49(10) which provides that references to assets of which a deceased person was competent to dispose are references to assets of the deceased which (otherwise than in right of a power of appointment or of the testamentary power conferred by statute to dispose of entailed interests) he could, if of full age and capacity, have disposed of by his Will, assuming that all the assets were situated in England, and if he was not domiciled in the United Kingdom, that he was domiciled in England, and include references to his severable share in any assets to which, immediately before his death, he was beneficially entitled as a joint tenant.

The definition covers most assets — other than trust property in which the deceased had an interest — but probably does not include a partnership share which was subject to an automatic accruer clause at the date of death.

The capital gains tax and inheritance tax elections are independent of each other.

Whether an election should be made depends on whether administration of the estate has been completed, and the rules are:

Administration of the estate completed

The point at which administration of an estate has been completed is not always obvious and the problem is dealt with at page 7. The general rule is that administration ends in relation to any particular asset when the personal representatives assent to a beneficiary or, if earlier, when residue is ascertained. For capital gains tax, if the administration of the estate has been completed, it is usually quite easy to decide whether the election should be made, bearing in mind that even if it is not, hold-over relief under FA 1980, s 79 should be available, provided that both donor and donee elect. Hold-over relief has the advantage that if any inheritance tax is payable on the variation (in other words, where no election is made under IHTA 1984, s 142(2)), it is allowable as a deductible expense for capital gains tax purposes on a subsequent disposal of the asset the subject of the variation, to the extent that it does not exceed the chargeable gain which would otherwise have arisen: s 79(5).

> *Example*
>
> X has died leaving his estate to his wife Y. The estate includes a valuable chargeable asset (worth £20,000) which Y wishes to pass on to her adult child, Z. She therefore enters into a written variation within two years after X's death, by which time the value of the asset has risen to £25,000. If an election is made under s 49(7), no gain will be realised on the variation and Z will be treated as acquiring the asset at £20,000. This could, of course, waste Y's annual capital gains tax exemption.
>
> On the other hand, if no election is made, Y will by the variation be disposing of the asset at market value at that time, making a gain of £5,000. The indexation allowance has been ignored for the purpose of this example. This may be within her annual exemption, depending on her other chargeable gains in the year. If her annual exemption is not available, Y and Z may elect to use hold-over relief under FA 1980, s 79 instead. The advantage of this is that if no election is made under IHTA 1984, s 142(2), the amount of any inheritance tax payable will increase the base cost for Z and if there have been costs of transferring the asset to Y beforehand, these too will increase Z's base cost. Indexation allowance will run from the date of the variation, however.

Administration of the estate continuing

However, if the administration of the estate has not been completed, the position is much more difficult. This is because the beneficiary of an unadministered estate has a *chose in action* which is no more than the right to compel proper administration of the estate, and the entire ownership of the property in the estate is in the deceased's legal personal representatives: *Commissioners of Stamp Duties (Queensland)* v *Livingston* [1965] AC 694. This right is valuable for inheritance tax purposes but is a separate asset from the estate property, for capital gains tax.

When the variation is made without a s 49(7) election, the variation will be a disposal by the original beneficiary of his *chose in action*, and it seems from CGTA 1979, s 29A that the original beneficiary's base cost of the *chose* (as opposed to the underlying assets) is nothing. Hold-over relief may therefore be necessary. Presumably, on completion of administration when the new beneficiary receives the assets he does not then dispose of the *chose* but it merges with the assets themselves. If this is correct, it saves a further capital gains tax problem, but if distribution does constitute a disposal by the new beneficiary, a further capital gains tax liability could arise.

> *Example*
>
> Using the same facts as in the example above, if when the variation is made by Y administration has not been completed and a s 49(7) election is made, the same consequences will apply as before, so that when the personal representatives distribute the asset to Z on completion of administration, he will acquire as legatee from them, at market value at the date of X's death.
>
> However, if no s 49(7) election is made in respect of the variation, when Z takes the asset on completion of administration the personal representatives then make a disposal to him (he is then not a legatee within the meaning of s 47(2)) and presumably they also make a gain, to which hold-over relief is then inapplicable, but their annual exemption may be available provided that administration is completed within two tax years after the tax year of death. The variation itself would presumably constitute a disposal of rights by Y but hold-over relief should be available. The complications and doubts that arise mean that it is generally worth making the election if administration has not been completed.

If an asset is showing a loss instead of a gain it may well be better to make a s 49(7) election so that the recipient takes over any unrealised loss. If no election is made the variation itself would give rise to a loss to the original beneficiary but any loss relief would be restricted if the disposal is to a connected person.

INCOME TAX

Income before variation

There are no specific relieving provisions for income tax when there has been a variation of the dispositions of a deceased's estate and the Revenue's view is simply that, following *Waddington* v *O'Callaghan* (1931) 16 TC 187, a deed cannot alter the past, so that income up to the date of the variation is taxed as that of the beneficiary entitled up to that date, even though that beneficiary might also have assigned the right to accrued but unpaid income. The rule does not apply to disclaimers and may not be applied if the variation is to rectify a defect or ambiguity in the Will. In each of these two cases the variation may be related back to the death. Otherwise, it is by no means certain that the Revenue view is correct on the income tax effect of a variation and it is worth considering briefly the position on the different types of legacy.

Pecuniary legacies

These carry interest at the rate of 6% per annum (The Rules of the Supreme Court (Amendment No 2) Order 1983) from the end of the executor's year to the date of payment, although on the spouse's statutory legacy on intestacy 6% per annum interest is payable from the date of death to the date of payment. Income tax is only payable if the interest is actually paid: *Dewar* v *IRC* (1935) 19 TC 561. It would therefore appear that if interest is paid to the assignee of a pecuniary legacy in respect of a period before a variation, the interest cannot be taxed as that of the assignor who has no title to it.

Specific gifts

If income arises from a specific gift, it is taxed as the income of the specific beneficiary as it arises, but only, apparently, by virtue of the doctrine of relation back on an assent being made: *IRC* v *Hawley* (1927) 13 TC 327, as to which see page 6. The Revenue take the view that this doctrine is so complete that the income before variation belongs to the original beneficiary even if he assigns the right to it. The point is, at least, debatable.

Limited interest in residue

The taxation of a beneficiary with a limited interest in residue (for example, a life interest) is governed by TA 1988, s 695 (s 426), which provides that sums paid to that beneficiary during the course of administration are deemed to be the income of that beneficiary for the tax year in which it was paid. On completion of administration, s 695(3) (s 426(3)) provides that sums paid and those due are deemed to have accrued to the beneficiary from day to day over the course of administration and are treated as income grossed up appropriately. The Revenue take the view that s 695(3) (s 426(3)) can apportion over a variation, so that the beneficiary who assigns his interest can nevertheless find that further sums are apportioned to him (or, presumably, away from him if he received too much). The Revenue view is not clearly supported by s 695 (s 426), and those for whom it is financially worthwhile should challenge it.

Absolute interest in residue

A beneficiary with an absolute interest in residue is taxed year by year on sums paid to him up to the amount of the residuary income (as defined in s 697 (s 428)). At the end of administration the beneficiary is treated as receiving the amount of the residuary income year by year: s 696(4) (s 427(4)). If a residuary beneficiary does not receive the full amount of residuary income before a variation, he can nevertheless find himself taxed on it on completion of administration.

Income tax anti-avoidance provisions

The income tax anti-avoidance provisions apply to 'settlements', which are defined to include any disposition, trust, covenant, agreement or arrangement and, in the case of TA 1988, s 663, (s 437), transfers of assets. In *IRC* v *Plummer* [1979] STC 793 it was confirmed that for the provisions to apply there must also be an element of bounty and in *Harvey* v *Sivyer* [1985] STC 434 it was held that an element of bounty must exist in relation to a disposition between parent and child even if made under a compulsion. It follows that a variation (but probably not a disclaimer) is an income tax settlement and thus subject to the anti-avoidance rules. This is particularly important when the variation has the effect of increasing the estate of the infant unmarried child of a party to the variation, or where s 683 (s 457) applies.

In *IRC* v *Buchanan* [1958] Ch 289, a fund was settled by Will on A for life with remainder to B for life with remainder to B's issue absolutely. A and B then surrendered their interests so that the fund became held for B's infant unmarried children. The Will trust itself was not a settlement within the anti-avoidance provisions (because it is impossible to treat income as that of a deceased person) but the surrender by B was held to be a disposition within the scope of s 663 (s 437), and B was assessed to tax on the settlement income. So if a surviving spouse wishes to redirect a deceased spouse's estate in favour of minor children, perhaps to make use of the deceased's nil rate band, the variation will be a s 663 (s 437) settlement even if it is an absolute gift because s 663 (s 437) also catches transfers of assets.

Where the variation is a result of genuinely compromised rights and not voluntary, it may be that the income tax anti-avoidance settlement provisions do not apply as a result of *Plummer*.

STAMP DUTY

Until 19 March 1985, *ad valorem* stamp duty was payable on written variations and it was often this that was the deciding factor in the choice between variations and disclaimers, since disclaimers were not liable to *ad valorem* stamp duty. *Ad valorem* stamp duty also led to multiple documents of variation, each coming within the £30,000 exemption — each document would not be part of a larger transaction because each was a gift: see for example *Kimber & Co* v *IRC* [1936] 1 KB 137.

For instruments executed on or after 19 March 1985 and stamped on or after 26 March 1985, *ad valorem* stamp duty on gifts was abolished by FA 1985, s 82. This covered most post-death rearrangements, but not those for a consideration, including a consideration of the making of a variation in respect of another of the dispositions. So FA 1985, s 84 provides that where, within the period of two years after a person's death any of the dispositions (whether effective by Will, under the law relating to intestacy or otherwise) the property of which he was competent to dispose are varied by an instrument executed by the persons or any of the persons who benefit or would benefit under the dispositions, stamp duty, under the heading 'Conveyance or Transfer on Sale' in Schedule 1 to the Stamp Act 1891 shall not be chargeable on the instrument. Section 84(2) provides that this does not apply where the variation is made for any consideration in money or money's worth other than consideration consisting of the making of a variation in respect of another of the dispositions. Accordingly, the exemption is in terms similar to those of capital gains tax and inheritance tax. The provisions are applicable whether or not administration of the estate is complete or the property has been distributed in accordance with the original dispositions: s 84(3).

A 50p stamp will be necessary if the document operates as a Conveyance or Transfer of property, and adjudication is necessary, but if the document is dated on or after 1 May 1987, it is exempt from stamp duty if appropriately certified under the Stamp Duty (Exempt Instruments) Regulations 1987. The Schedule to the Regulations has a list of categories and post-death variations qualify either as voluntary dispositions (category L) or if s 84 applies, under category M.

SUPPLEMENTARY BENEFITS

It may be that beneficiaries qualify for supplementary benefit and the receipt of the disposition on death would mean that their resources are increased and they cease to qualify for benefit. The question is whether a variation by such a beneficiary would be effective for supplementary benefit purposes so that the disposition is ignored and the benefit is not lost.

There are no special rules for post-death variations and supplementary benefit, but if a person deprives themself of a resource for the purpose of securing supplementary benefit or increasing the amount of such benefit, the resource may be treated as if it was still possessed by him. The benefit officer will consider the claimant's intention and it may be inferred from surrounding circumstances, before the discretion is exercised.

Whether an entitlement under an unadministered estate constitutes a resource for supplementary benefit purposes, is a matter of debate, but since it would appear to be a resource which is due and thus one which must be taken into account, it is likely that these self-deprivation rules apply.

JOINT TENANCY INTERESTS

A joint tenancy interest passes by survivorship, but it is clear that they are within the scope of IHTA 1984, s 142 and of the capital gains tax relief and can therefore be the subject of a variation.

Since the legal effect of a variation is a lifetime gift by the surviving joint tenant, even though for capital tax purposes it is treated as having been made by the deceased, it is within the power of the surviving joint tenant to make a gift of the joint tenancy interest inherited on the death and the gift would constitute the beneficiary of the variation a joint tenant with the survivor.

It has been argued that since the capital tax effect of the variation is that the deceased is treated as having made the disposition, the rule is inapplicable to joint tenancy interests because the deceased could not dispose of, nor sever, a joint tenancy interest by Will. But it is submitted that this is to confuse the capital tax consequence with the legal effect of the variation.

It is not possible to effect the gift of the joint tenancy interest by disclaimer since the result would be that the interest would pass back to the surviving joint tenant who was making the disclaimer in the first place.

For a variation of a joint tenancy interest, see precedent G.

NOMINATED PROPERTY

In certain cases power is given by statute to nominate property which passes by the nomination and not by Will or intestacy. Nominations once made cannot as a general principle be revoked by Will. The right to nominate has now been substantially curtailed, but nominations made before the date when the right was removed remain effective. For example, nominations of National Savings Bank Accounts made before 1 May 1981 are effective as are nominations of money in the Trustee Savings Bank made before 1 May 1979. The power to nominate money in a Friendly Society remains.

Nominated property forms part of the deceased's estate and is therefore within the scope of the inheritance tax or capital gains tax relief.

FORM OF VARIATION

Precedent A at page 55 and Precedent B at page 59 give the form of a standard written variation respectively of a Will and of an intestacy. However, the preliminary question needs to be considered as to whether a variation needs to be in writing or not and, if so, whether it should be by deed. For inheritance tax relief purposes, a variation must be in writing, but it is not in every case that inheritance tax relief will be sought. If no writing is required or used, there will be no document on which stamp duty will be leviable.

An individual who wishes to bind himself by a gratuitous promise must implement that promise by deed. A written variation will usually be a gratuitous promise to transfer assets or interests. However, a gift is effective if title is transferred to a donee and this can be done, for example, with cash and personal assets, by delivery without the need for writing — provided administration of the estate has ended. Other transfers, such as legal interests in shares and assignments of insurance policies, require writing in their own right. Until administration has ended, a beneficiary only has a *chose in action* whatever the nature of the asset and to transfer this probably requires writing by virtue of the Law of Property Act 1925, s 53(1)(*b*) or (*c*). It is likely that s 53(1)(*c*) will be the provision applicable to variations entered into before administration has ended, and thus require writing. Section 53(1)(*c*) provides that a disposition of an equitable interest or trust subsisting at the time of the disposition must be in writing and signed by the person disposing of the same or by his agent thereunto lawfully authorised in writing or by Will.

If writing is avoided by virtue of the nature of the asset and inheritance tax relief is not sought, the variation should take place only after administration has ended, or the 'donor' should use his own cash resources if, for example, he wishes to make the disposition earlier.

WHY VARY A WILL OR INTESTACY?

The principal reasons for rearranging dispositions under a Will or intestacy were given in Chapter I. Here is a selection of more detailed situations where it may be sensible to vary the dispositions of a Will or intestacy:

- To make gifts to chargeable beneficiaries, particularly children or issue, within the deceased's nil rate band:

  Example
  A dies leaving the whole of his estate of £300,000 to his wife, B. He also leaves two young children surviving; C and D, aged 15 and 12 respectively. B decides that she has more than enough to live on and would therefore like C and D to benefit from A's estate, not only simply to use up his nil rate band for inheritance tax, but also to ensure that her potential chargeable estate on her death is reduced. She therefore enters into a variation (making the appropriate election) whereby the children are given a £110,000, or whatever was the nil rate band at A's death, legacy on accumulation and maintenance trusts (she can be a trustee). It must be stressed that although no inheritance tax will be paid as a result of this variation, the variation is an income tax settlement by B and she will be taxed on distributed income until the children reach age 18.

- To provide the surviving spouse with extra funds to enable her to meet potentially exempt transfers during her lifetime.

  Example
  E dies in April 1988 leaving the whole of his £300,000 estate to his elderly wife F, who herself already has an estate of £300,000 (perhaps as a result of insurances maturing on E's death and a share in the matrimonial home) and a widow's pension. The potential inheritance tax bill on the £600,000 is £196,000. If, however, E's Will is varied so that £200,000 is given to chargeable beneficiaries — children or grandchildren, perhaps — and only £100,000 to F, leaving her with a total estate of £400,000, the inheritance tax payable on each estate will be £36,000 and £116,000 respectively, a total of £152,000 and a saving of £44,000 (entirely due to the use of the nil rate band on E's death). F can then reduce her estate by potentially exempt transfers.

It is very important indeed to note that if F's potentially exempt transfers do become chargeable on her death within seven years, then not only is the inheritance tax advantage lost (subject to tapering relief) but so is the capital gains tax uplift on those gifted assets which would here been given relief had F retained them. So potentially exempt transfers for the aged ought seriously to be thought about before making them.

A youngish surviving spouse can always dissipate substantial assets by making lifetime gifts (and surviving seven years, one hopes) and within her annual exemptions, so it may be better to vary £110,000, or the relevant nil rate band for the date of death, to chargeable beneficiaries on the first death.

- To skip a generation. Gifts to adults, including to the testator's adult children, can be redirected to their children or to an accumulation and maintenance trust for their children, thus passing over one generation to the next. This would only be done if the beneficiaries were reasonably well off and did not need the money, and the object is to avoid a potential inheritance tax charge arising when the beneficiaries would otherwise themselves pass on the property to their children.

- Where spouses die within two years of each other, to redirect benefits in such a way as to minimise the overall inheritance tax payable.

  Example
  G dies and leaves all his £200,000 estate to his wife H. She then dies within two years thereafter and leaves this £200,000 and her own £100,000 to their children. No inheritance tax is payable on G's death, but £76,000 is payable when H dies. If, however, H's personal representatives enter into a variation of G's Will whereby only £90,000 goes to H and £110,000 to the children, the effect is to reduce the total inheritance tax to £32,000. This saving can be greater for deaths when there were graduated rate bands.

- To give away increases in value inheritance tax free.

- To widen the administrative provisions applicable to Wills or on intestacy. For example, trustees of a Will Trust or on intestacy have their investment powers limited to those in the Trustee Investments Act 1961, unless, in the case of a Will, there is a wide investment clause. The beneficiary may wish to widen the trustees power of investment and also, perhaps, to include a provision enabling the trustees to provide a residence for a beneficiary. This can be done by a written variation, but if minor or unascertained beneficiaries are involved, only with Court consent under the Variation of Trusts Act 1958.

- To compromise potential claims under the Inheritance (Provision for Family and Dependants) Act 1975. As will be seen, certain persons are given the right to claim reasonable financial provision on the death of another and the disposition under an order is treated as being made by the deceased. However, if all concerned can agree how much should be provided for potential claimants, it is much cheaper and easier to redirect the benefits as agreed by a written variation. This can be effective for inheritance tax purposes only if made within two years after the relevant death. 1975 Act orders are, on the other hand, effective whenever made.

- Where the estate includes property which qualifies for agricultural relief or business property relief, that should generally be given by specific gifts to chargeable beneficiaries and not to exempt beneficiaries, to avoid wasting the relief. The special allocation of relief rules must be remembered, however, where there is an exempt beneficiary.

- It may be necessary to rearrange where the inheritance tax effect of IHTA 1984, ss 36–42 has a drastic result (see page 17). This provision should also be borne firmly in mind when actually making a variation in favour of chargeable beneficiaries.

III Disclaimers

WHAT IS A DISCLAIMER?

It is trite law, but remains as true now as when it was said by Abbot CJ in *Townson* v *Tickell* (1819) B & Ald 31 that 'The law certainly is not so absurd as to force a man to take an estate against his will'. A beneficiary under a Will or intestacy can, of course, disclaim an interest which would otherwise be taken. A disclaimer is thus a refusal to take an interest and in order to be able to disclaim, a beneficiary must not have 'accepted' the interest before disclaimer. Acceptance includes taking income from the gifted property or permitting it to be vested in the beneficiary's name, or taking any other form of benefit from it. Once a benefit has been accepted, it cannot be disclaimed.

A disclaimer is thus not a transfer of property rights, it is a refusal to accept them (*re Stratton's Disclaimer, Stratton* v *IRC* [1958] 1 Ch 42), and does not therefore require writing because the operation of a disclaimer is by way of avoidance and not a disposition within the scope of the Law of Property Act 1925, s 53: *re Paradise Motor Co* [1968] 2 All ER 625.

A disclaimer once made can be retracted, but only if it has not been acted on, and no other party has changed their position in reliance on it.

A beneficiary cannot disclaim part only of a single gift (*re Joel* [1943] Ch 311), but can disclaim one of two separate gifts given by Will. If it is anticipated that a beneficiary will wish to disclaim part of what has been given by Will, then separate gifts can be made to the same beneficiary, effectively enabling part disclaimers.

A precedent for a disclaimer is given on page 1.

EFFECT OF A DISCLAIMER

The effect of a disclaimer depends on the type of gift disclaimed, and is subject to any contrary intention expressed in the Will under which the disclaimer is made. A disclaimer cannot be made in favour of a specified person, and puts the donee, as regards his liabilities, burdens and rights, in the same position as if no gift had been made to him.

Specific gifts and pecuniary legacies

If a specific gift or pecuniary legacy is disclaimed, the property the subject of the legacy will form part of residue and thus pass to the residuary beneficiary. Thus if a legacy of £1,000 is disclaimed, the effect is that £1,000 no longer has to be found out of residue to repay it (assuming that the legacy is not charged on a specific asset) and the residuary beneficiary will take an extra £1,000. If a specific gift of an asset is disclaimed, that asset will simply form part of the testator's residuary estate.

Residuary gifts

If a gift of residue, or of a share of residue, is disclaimed, it will pass on intestacy. Thus if residue is left to the testator's two children A and B equally, and A disclaims his share, one half of residue will pass on the testator's intestacy. It may well be that A is also entitled to take on the testator's intestacy, and the disclaimer of a residuary interest does not operate as a disclaimer of an entitlement on intestacy. If residue is given to two or more beneficiaries as joint tenants, however, a disclaimer by one will pass that interest to the other or others (see below).

In most professionally drawn Wills, there will be a gift over of residue if the primary beneficiary fails to survive. The effect of a disclaimer of residue by a primary beneficiary in these circumstances depends on the wording of the gift over. If the gift over is made should the primary beneficiary not survive the deceased, a disclaimer by the primary beneficiary would not have the effect of passing residue to the beneficiaries of the gift over, since the primary beneficiary did not fail to survive the deceased, see eg, *re Sinclair* [1985] Ch 446. A disclaimer would have the effect of creating an intestacy. However, if the gift over of residue is made 'subject to' the gift to the primary beneficiary and without the requirement that the primary beneficiary should predecease the deceased, a disclaimer by the primary beneficiary would have the effect of passing residue on to the beneficiary of the gift over: re *Edwards Will Trusts* [1948] 1 Ch 440. The same applies where A disclaims a gift of residue which is given to him but it is provided that if the gift should fail for any reason, residue is to pass to B, B takes on a disclaimer. On the other hand, if the gift over is subject to the 'lapse' of the primary gift, a disclaimer by the primary beneficiary would not pass residue to the beneficiary of the gift over since a gift 'lapses' only if the beneficiary predeceased the testator.

Life interests
If a life interest, or right to income only, is disclaimed, the remainder falls in immediately. For example, if property is given to a surviving spouse for life with remainder to children if they attain the age of 25 and the surviving spouse disclaims her life interest, the property will be held for the children, subject to the contingency. However, if the remainder is given to take effect on the death of the life tenant, a disclaimer by the life tenant will create an intestacy over income until the death of the life tenant. Thus a gift of the life interest by variation would perhaps be more suitable.

Interests in remainder
If an interest in remainder in residue is disclaimed the general rule is that, on the death of the life tenant, the property which is the subject of the trust will pass on the original testator's intestacy.

Joint tenancy interests
If one of a number of joint tenants gives up his interest it will pass to the remaining joint tenant or tenants although it has been said (*obiter*) that this is not strictly a disclaimer: *re Schär* [1951] Ch 280. It is not thought that this is a point of any substance and a disclaimer by a joint tenant in these circumstances will be sufficient. Where there is only one surviving joint tenant, a disclaimer of the deceased's joint tenancy interest would have no effect. A variation is, however, possible: see p 28.

Intestacy
The effect of a disclaimer in relation to intestacy fell to be decided in re *Scott (deceased)* [1975] 2 All ER 1033. Walton J, in the second part of his judgment, had to determine in relation to a disclaimer of an interest under an intestacy whether the estate should be distributed to the Crown claiming it *bona vacantia*, or to those next entitled under the Administration of Estates Act 1925, s 46(1). He held that the person next entitled took. In relation to the estate, he said:

> 'Then the question comes, how is that to be disposed of? Well it is to be disposed of in accordance with the Administration of Estates Act 1925, but the executor has tried once to dispose of it and the intended beneficiaries have refused to accept it. What happens? It seems to me that the absolutely inevitable result, where all the members of one particular class have disclaimed, is to say: Very well, for the purposes of the distribution of the estate, that class must simply be left out of consideration.'

Presumably, where one member of a class disclaims, the remaining members of the class take. However, where the statutory trusts on intestacy apply, it is thought that a disclaimer by a child would not have the effect of passing that child's interest on to his or her own issue, but rather to the other members of that class — brothers and sisters — and if none, to those next entitled under the intestacy rules — parents of the intestate.

INHERITANCE TAX

The relief

IHTA 1984, s 17(*a*) and s 142(1) give relief from inheritance tax for disclaimers in a similar way to the relief given to written variations. The relevant parts of s 17(*a*) and s 142(1) states that where, within the period of two years after a person's death, the benefit conferred by any disposition by the deceased's Will or intestacy is disclaimed by an instrument in writing made by persons who benefit or would benefit under the dispositions, the disclaimer is not itself a transfer of value and inheritance tax is charged as if the disclaimed benefit had never been conferred.

Example

A dies leaving his share in the matrimonial home to his wife B and the residue of his estate to his two children, C and D equally. B does not wish to take the benefit of the matrimonial home and within two years of A's death disclaims the gift. As a result, the property forms part of residue and passes to C and D. The disclaimer is not a gift by B but A is treated as having given the property to C and D by his Will on his death. To take advantage of the inheritance tax relief, the disclaimer must be in writing.

No election needed

It is important to note that, unlike written variations, no election is required for these inheritance tax provisions to take effect and they therefore apply automatically. If, for other reasons, a disclaimer is to be made but the inheritance tax relief is not to be taken, the disclaimer should either be made otherwise than in writing or should be made over two years after the relevant death.

No consideration

As with written variations, a disclaimer is only effective for inheritance tax if it is consideration-free: s 142(3) and see page 13.

Other matters

The other provisions of s 142 apply to disclaimers as they do to written variations so, for example, the gifts with reservation rules do not apply. Nor does inheritance tax relief apply to an interest in possession owned by the deceased given by Will or intestacy.

Where a life interest is disclaimed, there is no time limit. IHTA 1984, s 93 provides that where a person becomes entitled to an interest in settled property but disclaims the interest, then if the disclaimer is not made for a consideration in money or money's worth, inheritance tax is levied as if he had not become entitled to the interest.

It is difficult to see how a disclaimer can successfully be made after administration of the estate has ended or the property concerned has been distributed, since both events imply acceptance of the relevant gift.

CAPITAL GAINS TAX

The relief
As for variations, capital gains tax relief is given for disclaimers by CGTA 1979, s 49(6). This provides that a disclaimer made within two years after a death is not a disposal and applies as if the disclaimed benefit had never been conferred. Unlike the provisions for variations, no election is required to give effect to this relief. The consequence is that the beneficiary who takes as a result of a disclaimer is treated as taking the disclaimed benefit as a legatee at the date of death. Because the operation of s 49(6) is automatic for disclaimers made within two years after a death, if it is desired that s 49(6) should not apply to a disclaimer, it must either be made more than two years after the death or it should be made otherwise than in writing: s 49(6) requires that the disclaimer should be in writing. If a beneficiary is to wait for two years before disclaiming a gift it may well be difficult to avoid accepting the gift in the meanwhile.

The considerations which have to be borne in mind when deciding whether to wait until the expiry of the two year period before making a disclaimer are similar to those which apply when deciding whether or not to make a s 49(7) election for a written variation (see page 16).

INCOME TAX

Income before disclaimer
As for variations, there are no specific provisions in the tax legislation to deal with disclaimers, so the normal rules apply. The effect of a disclaimer depends on the type of benefit disclaimed, bearing in mind that if a beneficiary who disclaims does in fact receive income, it will amount to acceptance of the gift and thus defeat the possibility of disclaimer.

Specific gifts and pecuniary legacies
It seems that the same rules as those which apply to written variations (page 25) are applied to disclaimers, so that the beneficiary who disclaims a specific gift can nevertheless find himself liable to income tax on the income arising up to the date of disclaimer even though he received none, but no liability should arise to a person who disclaims a pecuniary legacy. It is clear that if interest on a pecuniary legacy is disclaimed, the beneficiary disclaiming it is not liable to income tax on it: *Dewar* v *IRC* (1935) 19 TC 561.

Residuary gifts
The taxation of a beneficiary who disclaims a residuary gift depends on the nature of the interest disclaimed. If the interest disclaimed is a limited interest, the Revenue accept that the beneficiary who disclaims is *not* liable to income tax on income up to the date of disclaimer. If the interest disclaimed is an absolute interest, however, the Revenue practice is to assess the disclaiming beneficiary on the income up to the date of disclaimer. The rules are illogical but seem to be based on the estate duty case of *re Stratton's Disclaimer* (*supra*) which indicates that an interest remains in existence up to the date of a disclaimer.

Income after disclaimer
One major advantage of a disclaimer over a written variation is that the Revenue accept that a disclaimer does not constitute a 'settlement' so that the income tax anti-avoidance rules do not apply. Thus if the beneficiaries who take as a result of a disclaimer are the infant unmarried children of the disclaiming beneficiary, s 663 (s 437) will not operate.

STAMP DUTY

Because a disclaimer is not a transfer of property rights but rather a refusal to accept them, a disclaimer is not a conveyance or transfer operating as a voluntary disposition and is not liable to stamp duty even if effected by deed. The fixed 50p deed duty which used to apply to disclaimers was abolished by FA 1985.

WHY DISCLAIM?

In some circumstances where the dispositions of an estate are to be varied, it will be possible to achieve the same or similar results by a disclaimer and a written variation.

Example

E has died unmarried without issue or parents, leaving his property to such of his two sisters, F and G, as should survive him. G predeceased E leaving two minor children H and I, but because G fails to survive E, the gift to her lapses and F inherits the whole of residue. F wishes H and I to benefit and can achieve this either by a written variation or by disclaimer of her interest in residue. If she disclaims, E will then be treated as dying intestate over residue so that, as a result of the intestacy rules, F is entitled to one half of residue and H and I stand in G's shoes and are therefore entitled to the other half of residue contingent on reaching the age of 18 or on earlier marriage: Administration of Estates Act 1925, ss 46 and 47.

If a satisfactory solution can be produced by a disclaimer (and, in the above example, it may be that age 18 as a contingency is not satisfactory), the question arises which it is better to do: disclaim or vary. The differences are:

(1) A disclaimer is not treated as an income tax settlement; a written variation is.
(2) A disclaimer requires no election in order to be effective for inheritance tax and capital gains tax; a variation does.
(3) For inheritance tax, if more inheritance tax is payable as a result of a written variation, the personal representatives must join in; this does not apply to disclaimers.
(4) Where a life interest is to be disposed of, a disclaimer should not give rise to income tax for the disclaiming beneficiary; a variation may well do so.
(5) Where income tax is a problem for the disclaiming beneficiary, it may be better to have a written variation so that the original beneficiary can actually receive income to pay the income tax bill. The problem with disclaiming is that, by definition, the disclaiming beneficiary can receive no income from the disclaimed gift.
(6) If either or both inheritance tax and capital gains tax relief is *not* to be claimed, a written variation can be used within two years after the death without an election. A disclaimer must be made outside the two year period or should not be in writing.

But bear in mind:

(1) A disclaimer cannot be made in favour of a specified person, a variation can.
(2) A partial disclaimer is not possible.

IV Discretionary Wills

WHAT ARE THEY?

Some testators realise that the circumstances prevailing at their death could be very much different from those at the date of their Will and so wish their dispositions to be sufficiently flexible to be capable of taking changed circumstances into account. It would be unsatisfactory simply to leave it up to the beneficiaries to agree a change by written variation, either because the beneficiaries may not agree between themselves and, in any event, a Court order is needed for those who are unable to give their consent.

If flexibility is desired, there are two ways of building it into a Will. One is to empower executors or trustees to agree a variation on behalf of those who cannot consent, but this can still leave the decision whether to vary and, if so, how to do so, with adult beneficiaries along with the executors or trustees. The other solution is to have a discretionary Will under the terms of which a legacy or residue is given to the executors or nominated trustees on wide discretionary trusts over capital and income (including power to accumulate income) with dispositions in default of appointment after, say, 23 months, the default dispositions being those which the testator desires should take effect if circumstances remain unchanged. In this way the testator leaves it entirely up to his executors or nominated trustees to decide just what is best, and it goes without saying that he should therefore choose them with great care. It also obviates the need for consents on behalf of those who are unable to give their own consent.

This type of provision in a Will relies on the inheritance tax relief given to distributions out of discretionary trusts within two years after a death in IHTA 1984, s 144. A longer term discretionary trust can also be used.

Precedents D and E at pages 62 and 64 give respectively an appropriate discretionary trust clause and an appointment by the executors.

INHERITANCE TAX

Discretionary trusts by Will will usually be limited to a period slightly less than two years, but may alternatively be unlimited in time. Both can benefit from the relief given for distributions within two years after death. This is in IHTA 1984, s 144 which provides that where property comprised in a person's estate immediately before his death is settled by his Will and, within the period of two years after his death and before any interest in possession has subsisted in the property, an event occurs on which tax will be chargeable under the discretionary trust rules (other than the ten year charge) or would have been chargeable but for the exemption given to employees trusts, chargeable trusts or maintenance funds, then no tax is to be charged on the distribution and inheritance tax is levied as if the Will had provided that on the testator's death the property should be held as it is held after the event. No election to this effect is required.

Appointment before administration ends

One most important point to note is that inheritance tax will have to be paid on the trust fund on application for a Grant of Probate whether or not there is a surviving spouse in whose favour it is intended to make an appointment if the discretion has not already been exercised. Prima facie, the trustees will not be able to exercise their powers until administration has been completed and it will not be until then that tax can be recovered in respect of property appointed to a surviving spouse, although interest at the appropriate rate will be carried by tax repayments. In order to avoid the problem of having to pay tax before Grant of Probate, it is usually provided that trustees may exercise their powers before obtaining probate and also before administration is completed. They can then exercise their powers before the grant in favour of the surviving spouse and no inheritance tax will be payable on the appointed property. The Revenue's view on this appears to be that, if expressly authorised, the exercise of the power before the end of administration is effective as regards personal income. However, what the trustees are appointing is a *chose in action* which arises at the date of death.

The first three months

In many cases it will be intended that the surviving spouse is to be the primary beneficiary and the executors will wish to exercise their discretion accordingly as soon as possible. However, there is a trap. The relieving provisions in s 144 do not apply if the relevant appointment is made within three months after the death. This is because s 144 only applies if it would otherwise be chargeable, and an appointment out of a discretionary trust within three months after creation is not chargeable.

It may be that the surviving spouse has financial difficulties and three months is too long to wait. One solution would be to give the spouse a separate pecuniary legacy to tide him or her over the initial period and as soon as the three months are up, an appointment can be made. Obviously, grant should not be sought in the meanwhile, or inheritance tax would become payable.

Long term trusts

Relief under s 144 is given only if the event occurs within two years after the death so if the testator wishes to be certain that the trustees will take advantage of the relief, default gifts must be provided by the Will and must arise automatically within this period. If the trusts are not limited to the two year period the trustees may consider waiting until just before the ten year anniversary before distributing the property. Distributions outside the initial two year term will be subject to the normal inheritance tax exit charge which is calculated by cumulating the value of the settled property at the date of the testator's death (including the value of related settlements — other settlements under the same Will IHTA 1984, s 62) with the deceased's lifetime chargeable transfers within the seven years before death, and is levied at three-tenths of the relevant lifetime rates, multiplied by one-fortieth for every completed quarter since the date of death. It will readily be appreciated that the maximum possible rate of inheritance tax since the budget is 6% (three-tenths × the maximum lifetime rate of 20%) and if the settled property was within the settlor's nil rate band available at death, the rate would be zero. In many cases, therefore, a distribution before the first ten year anniversary outside the initial two year term can be fiscally advantageous. The charge at the ten year anniversary is levied on values at that time and on the then current rates of tax, and it is usually advantageous to distribute before the anniversary occurs because the exit charge is based on values at the date of creation.

Nil rate band discretionary trusts

Discretionary trusts over a nil rate band legacy only, have two main advantages. First, they give flexibility, albeit over an amount less than the whole of the estate; secondly, no inheritance tax is payable whether or not the discretion is exercised before grant or, indeed, within the first two years provided that the deceased has made no lifetime chargeable transfers or potentially exempt transfers in the seven years before death. This eventuality can be catered for as can changes in the nil rate band from time to time, and an appropriate precedent is given at the end of Precedent D. The amount of the gift depends on the amount available of the testator's nil rate at the date of death and is therefore reduced by lifetime chargeable transfers including potentially exempt transfers which become chargeable, made within the previous seven years. Once the nil rate band discretionary trust has been set up, then at least until the ten year anniversary, there will be no charge if property leaves the trust provided that no other trusts are created by the Will. For example, if the Will gives the surviving spouse a life interest in residue, then in calculating the rate of tax on exit for the nil rate band discretionary trust, the value of the life interest fund at the date of the death must be taken into account because it is a related settlement as defined by s 62. This would clearly defeat the long-term purpose of the nil rate band discretionary trust and the trustees must consider the position carefully before a two year period has elapsed.

Life interests followed by discretionary trusts

As mentioned at p 15, the capital in a life interest fund is outside the scope of s 142. There is an additional problem, F(No 2)A 1987, Sched 7 introduced into IHTA, 1984, s 54A, anti-avoidance rules which apply where the settlor created a life interest which is then converted into discretionary trusts within seven years and while the settlor is still alive. Section 54A provides that the applicable rate of tax is the higher of that of the settlor and that of the life tenant. The provision is clearly aimed at those who indirectly try to set up discretionary trusts using the much lower rate of tax of the life tenant. However, Sched 7 also applies if the life tenant inadvertantly dies within the seven year period and the life interest is followed by discretionary trusts. There is therefore a relieving provision in s 54A(2)(d) whereby the anti-avoidance rules in s 54A do not apply to the extent that within six months after to the coming to an end of the interest in possession, the property in which that interest subsisted has become subject to a qualifying interest in possession, or to accumulation and maintenance trusts, or an individual has become beneficially entitled.

The Revenue has also stated that relief is available under s 144 where the deceased life tenant was given by the Settlement a general power of appointment which is exercisable and exercised by his Will so as to create discretionary trusts. Any distribution by the trustees within two years after the death of the life tenant will be within the scope of s 144.

CAPITAL GAINS TAX

There is nothing in the capital gains tax legislation which specifically deals with an appointment of property out of a discretionary Will trust, so the normal settlement rules apply. Thus, if the appointment is to be to a beneficiary absolutely, the trustees will at the date of the appointment be treated as disposing of the trust property and immediately reacquiring it as bare trustees, at market value: CGTA 1979, s 54. However, if a trust interest is created by the appointment, there is no disposal and reacquisition unless a separate settlement is created. This is often a difficult question to answer and the Revenue's Statement of Practice in the area, SP 7/84 gives guidelines.

However, if capital gains tax would otherwise arise, there are two reliefs which may help. The first is that trustees have an annual exemption of one half of that given to individuals, although if executors as such are exercising the power, the full annual exemption may be available. The second relief is more important and is that on disposals by trustees to beneficiaries or by trustees to trustees, capital gains tax can be held over under FA 1980, s 79 and FA 1982, s 82, provided that both disponor and recipient agree.

What this all means, then, is that capital gains tax should not be a problem on an appointment out of a discretionary Will trust, and this seems to be so whether the appointment is made before or after the estate has been administered.

INCOME TAX

The trusts over income will be discretionary so that it cannot be said that any beneficiary is entitled to the income unless it is distributed in the exercise of the discretion. The additional rate of tax should not be payable by the personal representatives since FA 1973, ss 16 and 17 do not apply to personal representatives. Thus a beneficiary who receives income before the assets are appointed will be liable to be taxed on the sum received, grossed up at the basic rate under TA 1988, s 695, (s 426). After the appointment is made, income arising is taxed under the normal rules, at the basic rate (currently 25%) and additional rate (currently 10%).

Unlike post death variations, appointments by trustees do not create income tax settlements.

STAMP DUTY

The appointment of property from the discretionary trust bears a 50p duty only as a 'Conveyance or Transfer of any kind', unless certified as exempt under the Stamp Duty (Exempt Instruments) Regulations 1987. The relevant category for such appointments is F.

V Other rearrangements

PRECATORY TRUSTS

What are they?
In order to create a binding trust, three certainties must exist: certainty of words, subject matter and objects: *Knight* v *Knight* (1840) 3 Beav 148. An obvious example of all three certainties is a gift of Whiteacre to A and B on trust for C for life with remainder to D. To have certainty of words means that the words creating the trust must be imperative, and in the foregoing example the words 'on trust' are sufficient. If words used are not sufficiently imperative, the absence of certainty of words means that the trust fails. Such words are precatory words and include those indicating hope, wishes or confidence. An example is given in the case of *re Conolly* [1910] 1 Ch 219 where a gift by Will was made to the testator's sisters equally, with the words 'I specifically desire that the sums hereby bequeathed shall . . . be specifically left by the legatees to such charitable institutions . . . as my sisters may select and in such proportions as they determine'. The word 'desire' was insufficiently imperative and the gift took effect as an absolute gift to the sisters.

Thus the use of precatory words does not create a binding trust and, where precatory words are used in this way, the gift is called a precatory trust even though the expression is a contradiction in terms. So if a testatrix leaves her jewellery to one of her children coupled with the request that that child should distribute the jewellery between all the issue of the testatrix as fairly as possible, the use of precatory words means that the gift is an absolute gift of the jewellery to the named child. It is then up to that child whether or not he or she acts in accordance with the wishes of the testatrix.

Why have one?
Precatory trusts are most often used in relation to chattels, particularly jewellery, where the assets owned by the testator or testatrix may change, or he or she may not have decided who should get what. To ensure a binding trust, every change would require a new Will or codicil, which is impractical. The simple solution is therefore to create a precatory trust, and instructions to the named

(and well-trusted) beneficiary can be amended as appropriate from time to time, generally by letter or some other informal memorandum. The result is flexibility and simplicity — the Will does not have to include a long list of the chattels to be distributed. An example of a precatory trust might be:

> 'I GIVE AND BEQUEATH all my personal chattels as defined by section 55(1)(*x*) of the Administration of Estates Act 1925 to [my wife] for her own absolute use and benefit and I express the wish (but without imposing any legal obligation on her) that she should distribute such assets in accordance with any instructions I communicate to her whether orally or in writing.'

If the gift is to be jewellery, for the words 'personal chattels as defined by section 55(1)(*x*) of the Administration of Estates Act 1925' should be substituted the words 'jewellery including rings earrings necklaces bracelets brooches and watches'.

Inheritance tax

The named beneficiary is treated as owning absolutely all the property which is the subject of the precatory trust and that property is therefore part of his estate and if he then distributes in accordance with the request, the effect is that his estate is reduced and inheritance tax has to be considered. If tax were to be charged immediately or potentially in these circumstances, or annual exemptions or the nil rate band used up in whole or in part, it might encourage the named beneficiary to keep the gifted property and not act in accordance with the testator's wishes. However, there are relieving provisions in IHTA 1984, ss 17(*b*) and 143 which provide that where a testator expresses a wish that property bequeathed by his Will should be transferred by the legatee to other persons, and the legatee transfers any of the property in accordance with that wish within the period of two years after the death of the testator —

(*a*) the transfer shall not be a transfer of value, and

(*b*) the Act shall have effect as if the property transferred had been bequeathed by the Will to the transferee.

Note that the request does not have to be included in the Will. It is understood to be the Revenue practice that the request 'should have been made in terms sufficiently certain for the Court to have given effect to it had it been binding'.

Sections 17(*b*) and 143 mean that there should be no adverse inheritance tax consequences if the beneficiary does as requested by a testator, provided that he does so within two years after the death and the property concerned is personalty. It is not clear whether the provisions apply to real property since there is only a reference to property 'bequeathed' and not to property 'devised'. Since it is highly improbable that real property will be subject to such gift anyway, the point is considered to be of little significance. That having been said, however, there was a report in the Sunday papers on 29 July 1984 that a Somerset farmer had left his £2m estate, including realty, to his secretary, who had announced that she would act in accordance with the testator's wishes and put all the property into a trust to keep the testator's five farms and sixty workers going. If, as is quite possible, the provisions do not apply to realty, the secretary will have found the exercise not a little expensive, unless she had waited until the introduction of inheritance tax and made a potentially exempt transfer.

The position on the reservation of benefit rules for precatory trusts is perfectly clear. The relieving provision is that where property is transferred in accordance with the testator's wishes, the 1984 Act shall have effect as if the property transferred had been bequeathed by the Will to the transferee and so transfers by the legatee are to be treated as transfers by a nominee or bare trustee and are thus not 'gifts' within the scope of the 1984 Act. The rules, therefore, do not apply.

Capital gains tax

There is no specific provision in the capital gains tax legislation giving relief where a beneficiary acts in accordance with the testator's wishes under a precatory trust. Presumably, the beneficiary can only distribute the assets once he has received them and thus only after administration has ended in relation to those assets. So if a beneficiary does give effect to a precatory trust, each distribution will be a disposal by that beneficiary and if the relevant asset shows a gain from the date of death, capital gains tax could be payable. There are a number of reliefs, however, which should mean that capital gains tax is not a problem. These reliefs include hold over relief under FA 1980, s 79 (but only if the recipient agrees), relief for gains made on disposals of chattels where the amount or value of the consideration for the disposal does not exceed £3,000, indexation and the annual capital gains tax exemption.

Income tax

If any income from a specific gift arises before the beneficiary acts in accordance with the testator's wishes, that income will be taxed in the same way as that of any other specific beneficiary up to the date of the gift (see page 25).

Stamp Duty

Chattels are transferable by delivery, so no stamp duty should be levied. If, exceptionally, other assets are transferred, a 50p duty will be leviable and adjudication required, unless the document can be approximately certified (see p 27).

CAPITALISATION OF LIFE INTEREST ON INTESTACY

The election

When a person dies intestate, leaving a spouse and issue, the surviving spouse is entitled to the deceased's personal chattels, a statutory legacy of £75,000 with interest at 6% from the date of death to payment, and a life interest in half of the remainder.

The trustees who hold property on trust for the surviving spouse for life have no power to distribute capital to that spouse and (apart from selling the interest or breaking the trust under the rule in *Saunders* v *Vautier*, as to which see page 8) the only way in which the spouse can obtain a capital sum instead of the life interest is to elect to capitalise it under the provisions of the Administration of Estates Act 1925, s 47A.

The method of calculating the capital sum to be given to the surviving spouse in lieu of income is laid down by AEA 1925, s 47A(2) as amended by the Administration of Justice Act 1977, s 28 and the Intestate Succession (Interest and Capitalisation) Order 1977 (SI 1977 No 1491). The value is found by multiplying the trust fund by a decimal fraction given in the Order, which fraction varies according to age and sex of the surviving spouse. The effect will be that the capital sum taken will be less than that in which the life interest subsisted. The balance of the property in which the life interest subsisted will thereafter be held for issue on the statutory trusts. The election should generally be made within twelve months after the date of grant, by the surviving spouse to the personal representative.

Inheritance tax

If there were no relieving provisions, the effect of the election would be that the surviving spouse would be giving up an interest in possession in the whole of the trust fund and receiving an absolute interest in part only, so that the election would operate as a transfer of value by the surviving spouse, the gift being made to issue. However, IHTA 1984, ss 17(*c*) and 145 provide that an election by a surviving spouse under AEA 1925, s 47A, is not a transfer of value and inheritance tax is to be charged as if the surviving spouse had not been entitled to the life interest, but had been entitled to the capital sum instead. There is no time limit laid down in ss 17(*c*) and 145, apart from that implicit as a result of AEA 1925, and the inheritance tax result is automatic — no election is available.

The inheritance tax result of the capitalisation is, therefore, that:

(1) the termination of the interest in possession by the surviving spouse is not subject to inheritance tax; and
(2) since the capital value taken by the surviving spouse will be less than the value of the trust fund in which the life interest subsisted, the amount of the deceased's estate qualifying for the spouse exemption will be less and the chargeable estate passing to the issue will be greater. This can increase the inheritance tax bill.

Depending on the circumstances, and provided that the issue are of full age, it may be better to divide up the fund under the rule in *Saunders* v *Vautier*, other than by a s 142(1) variation, or even by a written variation without an election (as to which, see page 16), so that the surviving spouse is treated as making the transfer of value of the extra sum, and not the intestate but bear in mind the reservation of benefit rules (page 13). Such a distribution can of course be a potentially exempt transfer.

ORDERS UNDER THE INHERITANCE (PROVISION FOR FAMILY AND DEPENDANTS) ACT 1975

1975 Act provisions

Where a deceased dies domiciled in England and Wales, application may be made under the Inheritance (Provision for Family and Dependants) Act 1975 by:

(1) a wife or husband of the deceased;
(2) a former wife or former husband of the deceased who has not remarried;
(3) a child of the deceased;
(4) any person (not being a child of the deceased) who, in the case of any marriage to which the deceased was at the time a party, was treated by the deceased as a child of the family in relation to that marriage; or
(5) any person (not being a person included in the foregoing) who immediately before the death was being maintained, either wholly or partly, by the deceased.

Application may be made on the ground that the deceased's Will or the law relating to intestacy, or a combination, does not make reasonable financial provision for the applicant. The application must be made to the Court within six months after the date of grant and the

Court has a discretion (rarely exercised) to extend that time limit. The Court is directed by s 3 to have regard through a number of matters in exercising its powers, such as the financial resources and needs of the applicant and of the other beneficiaries.

Section 2 gives the Court power to make one or more of the following orders to be satisfied out of the deceased's net estate:

(1) a periodical payments order for such term as may be specified;
(2) a lump sum order;
(3) a transfer of property order;
(4) a settlement of property order;
(5) an acquisition of property order; and
(6) an order varying an anti-or post-nuptial settlement.

Section 8 lays down what property is to be treated as part of the deceased's net estate, including nominated property and property the subject of a *donatio mortis causa*. Further, by s 9, the Court has power to order that joint tenancy interests should form part of the net estate. By s 10, the Court has power to set aside dispositions intended to defeat applications for financial provision, made by the deceased within six years before death, and by s 11 certain contracts to leave property by Will can be set aside. Orders under ss 10 and 11 have the effect of increasing the net estate of the deceased. Under ss 8, 9 and 10, the Court is directed to have regard to the amount of tax payable in respect of the property the subject of the order.

Finally, s 19(1) provides that:

> Where an order is made under section 2 of this Act then for all purposes, including the purposes of the enactments relating to capital transfer tax, the will or the law relating to intestacy, or both the will and the law relating to intestacy, as the case may be, shall have effect and be deemed to have had effect as from the deceased's death subject to the provisions of the order.

Section 19 thus does not apply to property such as nominated property, joint property and property the subject of a *donatio mortis causa*, which passes otherwise and than by Will or intestacy, nor does it apply to a s 10 order.

Inheritance tax

The provisions of s 19 of the 1975 Act are duplicated and extended by IHTA 1984, s 146, which applies to deaths on or after 6 April 1976. Section 146 provides that property forming part of the net estate of a deceased which is subject to an order under s 2 of the 1975 Act shall for inheritance tax purposes be treated as if it had devolved on the death in accordance with the provisions of the order.

This therefore includes nominated property, joint property and property that is subject to a *donatio mortis causa*. Section 10 orders are also dealt with (see below).

The effect of a 1975 Act order is, of course, to benefit an applicant at the expense of one or more beneficiaries, and s 146 scotches any potential argument about whether the reduction in the beneficiary's estate at the time of the order constitutes a transfer of value by the beneficiary who loses. However, it may be that the amount of inheritance tax payable in respect of the death varies, for example, where an order is made in favour of a surviving spouse. In this case, if inheritance tax has been paid, the refund will be repaid to the personal representatives (s 146(4)).

If an order is made setting aside a lifetime gift by the deceased, s 146(2), (3) and (5) provide that the deceased's personal representatives may reclaim any inheritance tax paid on that lifetime gift, whoever paid it, and the deceased's estate rate is to be calculated without regard to the value transferred by the lifetime gift. This is fair, because if the donee paid the inheritance tax, the order under s 10 will only relate to the amount net of inheritance tax, and the donee will therefore not lose. However, it must be remembered that the value of the gifts set aside will (with the inheritance tax reclaimed) be part of the deceased's estate and liable for inheritance tax at the death rates, except to the extent that it passes to an exempt beneficiary. Further, since the advent of inheritance tax, the number of lifetime gifts on which tax will actually have been paid, will reduce very considerably.

Where settlements are varied or terminated under the 1975 Act, IHTA 1984, s 146(6) provides that the variation or termination is not chargeable to inheritance tax.

It will be noted that these relieving provisions only apply to orders made under ss 2 or 10 of the 1975 Act, but consent orders qualify under s 146(8). This provides that where an order is made staying or dismissing proceedings under the 1975 Act on terms set out in or scheduled to the order, s 146 shall have effect as if any of those terms which could have been included in an order under s 2 or s 10 of that Act were provisioned of such an order. Bear in mind that for s 146(8) to take effect, there must be an order. Often, potential family provision claims are compromised without recourse to the courts. If this happens, the compromise must be within two years after the death if inheritance tax and capital gains tax relief is to be used.

The reservation of benefit rules in TA 1986, s 102 are irrelevant since there is highly unlikely to be any gift element.

Capital gains tax

There is no specific relieving provision in the Capital Gains Tax Act 1979 for 1975 Act orders, but the general provisions of s 19 of the 1975 Act (see above) would seem to apply, so that orders made under s 2 will, as it were, be back-dated to the date of death for capital gains tax, and thus no disposal will arise at the date of the order.

As has already been noted, s 19 does not apply to orders in relation to nominated property, joint property and property the subject of a *donatio mortis causa*, and s 19 does not apply to s 10 orders, in which case the order may well result in a disposal by the relevant beneficiary of his interest in the property concerned, with capital gains tax payable. Section 49(6), (as to which see page 22), however, does apply to property of which the deceased was competent to dispose provided the disposition was effected 'by will, under the law relating to intestacy *or otherwise*', so if the order is made within two years of death and the appropriate election made, then to the extent that there is a potential liability capital gains tax could be avoided, except possibly in relation to property the subject of a *donatio mortis causa* and s 10 orders.

Income tax

As for capital gains tax, s 19 of the 1975 Act, would seem to apply to income tax and therefore the s 2 order will be treated as being made as at the date of death. In *re Pointer* [1946] Ch 324, for example, it was held that an order under the Inheritance (Family Provision) Act 1938 was effective from death and was to be treated as made on death. The 1938 Act contained a provision similar to s 19 of the 1975 Act.

If this is correct, s 19 is the only provision which specifically deals with income tax in relation to post-death rearrangements, and the effect is presumably that the original beneficiary will not be liable to income tax on any property given to him and which is subsequently the subject of an order under the 1975 Act, whereas the person in whose favour the order is made is treated as receiving the benefit on the date of death and the usual income tax provisions, for example, under TA 1988, s 695 and s 696, (ss 426 and 427) (see page 26) will be applied to the successful 1975 Act applicant as from the date of death.

Deed of Variation of a Will

THIS DEED OF VARIATION is made the . . . . day of . . . . .

198 . . . . BETWEEN [AB] of . . . .

. . . . (hereinafter called ['Mrs B']) of the one

part and [CD] of . . . .

. . . . and [EF] of

. . . .

. . . . (hereinafter together called 'the Trustees') of the other part

WHEREAS

(A) [BB] (hereinafter called 'the Testator') died on . . . . having made his last Will (hereinafter called 'the Will') dated the . . . . day of . . . . whereby he appointed the Trustees to be the executors and trustees thereof

(B) On the . . . . day of . . . . the Trustees obtained a grant of Probate of the Will out of the Principal [.................... District] Registry of the Family Division
[No grant of Probate of the Will has yet been obtained by the Trustees]

(C) By Clause 3 of the Will the Testator directed the Trustees to hold the residue of his estate on trust either to sell it or (if they thought fit and without being liable for loss) to retain all or any part of it and to pay debts funeral and testamentary expenses and to hold the balance upon trust for [Mrs B] absolutely provided that she should survive him by a period of twenty-eight days

(D) [Mrs B] is desirous of varying the disposition of the Will for the benefit of her children and issue as hereinafter appears

NOW THIS DEED WITNESSETH as follows:

1. The dispositions by the Will shall hereby be varied and the Will shall be read and construed in all respects as if it had contained the following provisions in addition to the provisions therein contained:

'A. I GIVE AND BEQUEATH the sum of [£50,000 (fifty thousand pounds)] unto my Trustees UPON TRUST to hold the same for such of my children as shall attain the age of thirty years and if more than one in equal shares absolutely PROVIDED THAT if any of my said children shall predecease me or shall survive me but die before attaining a vested interest leaving issue surviving him or her such issue as shall attain the age of twenty-one years shall take if more than one in equal shares per stirpes the share which such deceased child would have taken had he or she survived to take a vested interest but so that no issue shall take whose parent is alive and so capable of taking and this gift shall carry the intermediate income and SUBJECT THERETO the said sum or investments representing it shall be held UPON TRUST for [charity or other named beneficiary] absolutely

B. Sections 31 and 32 of the Trustee Act 1925 shall apply hereto but subject to the following variations:

   1. the said Section 31 shall have effect as if the words 'my Trustees think fit' were substituted in sub-section (1)(i) thereof for the words 'may in all the circumstances be reasonable' and as if the proviso at the end of sub-section (1) thereof were omitted and as if the age of twenty-one were substituted for the age of eighteen and infant and infancy shall be construed accordingly
   2. the said Section 32 shall have effect as if the words 'advancement maintenance education or benefit' were substituted for the words 'advancement or benefit' wherever the same appear and as if the words 'one half of' were omitted from proviso (*a*) to sub-section (1) thereof

C. IN ADDITION to the powers given to them by law my Trustees shall have the following powers exercisable at their discretion:

   1. power to invest any money in such manner and in such part of the world as my Trustees may think fit and (in particular) in the making of loans whether or not at interest and with or without security and the purchase or improvement of a freehold or leasehold dwelling for use as residence by any beneficiary hereunder
   2. power to vary or transpose any investment into or for any other or others of any nature herein authorised or to vary the terms of or property comprised in any security
   3. power to insure any property subject to the trusts hereof against such risks as my Trustees shall think fit with power to pay premiums out of income or capital

4. power to permit any beneficiary to reside in any freehold or leasehold dwellinghouse subject to the trusts of this Will and in which such beneficiary shall have a vested or contingent interest whether present or future with power for my Trustees to make such arrangements as they shall think fit for the payment of outgoings and expenses in respect of such dwellinghouse and the indemnity of my Trustees against any liabilities in connection therewith and with power to apply the income or capital of any of the property held subject to the same trusts as such dwellinghouse for such purposes or any of them

[Here also insert other administrative provisions as desired, such as the power to borrow, power to maintain property used as a residence, a receipt clause and a charging clause]

2. The parties hereto hereby give notice to the Board of Inland Revenue in accordance with Section 142(2) of the Inheritance Tax Act 1984 and Section 49(7) of the Capital Gains Tax Act 1979 that the provisions of Section 142(1) and Section 49(6) thereof respectively shall apply to this variation

3. It is certified that this instrument falls within category L in the Schedule to the Stamp Duty (Exempt Instruments) Regulations 1987

IN WITNESS whereof the parties hereto have hereunto set their hands and seals the day and year first before written

SIGNED SEALED and DELIVERED

by the said [AB] . . . . L.S.

in the presence of:

. . . .

[Signature of witness]

of . . . .

[Address of witness]

SIGNED SEALED AND DELIVERED

by the said [CD] . . . . L.S.

in the presence of:

. . . .

SIGNED SEALED and DELIVERED

by the said [EF] . . . . L.S.

in the presence of

. . . .

NOTES

1. No Stamp duty is required, and the document cannot be submitted to the Revenue for stamping or adjudication. If the stamp duty certificate is not contained in the document, it may be endorsed on it or firmly attached to it if prepared separately. The certificate must be signed by the transferor, or by a solicitor on behalf of the transferor. An authorised agent of the transferor who is not a solicitor may also sign provided he states the capacity in which he signs, confirms that he is authorised and that he has knowledge of the fact of the transaction.
2. The deed will be a settlement by Mrs B on her infant unmarried children and will thus be caught by TA 1988, s 663, (s 437) (see page 26). It will also be caught by TA 1988, s 683 (s 457) (excess liability) unless a gift over to charity or other named beneficiary than Mrs B, is included.
3. The £50,000 legacy will not involve the payment of any extra inheritance tax if the deceased's nil rate band was still intact. If not, inheritance tax will become payable by the Trustees if cumulative chargeable transfers exceeded £60,000 (for deaths after 14 March 1988). The Trustees should ensure that they have sufficient resources to meet this testamentary expense out of residue. If, alternatively, it is desired to impose the burden of inheritance tax on the legacy, the words 'subject to inheritance tax' should be inserted after the words 'GIVE AND BEQUEATH' on the first line of Clause A. No covenant with the trustees to pay the tax is necessary if they still hold the estate and have sufficient resources to meet the liability. If administration has been completed, the Trustees will presumably have no resources for tax, but in this event, they do not have to join into the deed nor into the election. Provided that the trustees have obtained a discharge in Form 30 (s 239), the liability for any further tax is that of the beneficiary.
4. If inheritance tax is leviable on the legacy, bear in mind the grossing up problems (see p 17).
5. As to whether an election is desirable, see page 16.
6. The trusts for the children are accumulation and maintenance trusts up to age 21 as a result of Clause B1.

Deed of Variation on Intestacy

THIS DEED OF VARIATION is made the .... day of............

198...........BETWEEN [GH] of ....

.... (hereinafter called ['Mrs H'])

of the one part and [HH] of ....

.... hereinafter called ['Miss H']) of the other part

WHEREAS

(A) [IH] (hereinafter called 'the Deceased') died on.................................... intestate leaving surviving him [Mrs H] who was his lawful wife and [Miss H] who is his only child and who has attained the age of eighteen years

(B) By virtue of the Administration of Estates Act 1925 as amended [Mrs H] as surviving spouse is entitled to the personal chattels of the Deceased and in addition to a legacy of £75,000 (seventy-five thousand pounds) and interest thereon and subject thereto the residuary estate of the Deceased is held as to one half upon trust for [Mrs H] during her life and subject thereto the residuary estate is held for [Miss H] absolutely

(C) [Mrs H] and [Miss H] obtained a grant of letters of administration to the estate on .... out of the Principal [................... District] Registry of the Family Division

(D) [Mrs H] and [Miss H] being the persons together solely entitled to all the real and personal property comprised in the estate of the Deceased passing under his intestacy (which estate is hereinafter called 'the Estate') are desirous of varying the dispositions thereof as hereinafter appears

NOW THIS DEED WITNESSETH and it is hereby agreed as follows:

1. That the dispositions of the Estate shall be varied and take effect as if the Deceased had made the following dispositions of his Estate at the date of his death, namely:
   (*a*) a pecuniary legacy of [£30,000 (thirty thousand pounds)] free of inheritance tax to be paid to [Miss H] absolutely and subject thereto

(*b*) the Estate shall be held on trust for [Mrs H] absolutely

2. The parties hereto being the persons making this instrument and the personal representatives of the Deceased hereby give notice to the Board of Inland Revenue in accordance with Section 142(2) of the Inheritance Tax Act 1984 and Section 49(7) of the Capital Gains Tax Act 1979 that the provisions of Section 142(1) and Section 49(6) thereof respectively shall apply to this variation
3. Stamp Duty Precedent, as in Precedent A

IN WITNESS etc.

NOTES

1. If IH had made previous *inter vivos* chargeable transfers so that inheritance tax was payable in the £30,000 legacy; the grossing up and attribution provisions in IHTA 1984, ss 36–42 must be remembered, see page 17.
2. No stamp duty or adjudication is requested.
3. The statutory legacy for the surviving spouse on intestacy where the intestate left issue, was increased from £40,000 to £75,000 with effect for deaths from 1 June 1987. The statutory legacy for surviving spouse where the intestate left no issue, but was survived by parents or brothers and sisters of the whole blood or their issue, was increased from £85,000 to £125,000.

Deed of Disclaimer

THIS DEED OF DISCLAIMER is made the ______________ day of ______

198____ BY [IJ] of ______________________________

WHEREAS

(A) [JJ] (hereinafter called 'the Testator') died on ____________ having made his last Will (hereinafter called 'the Will') on ____________

(B) By clause ____ of the Will the Testator gave a pecuniary legacy of [£20,000 (twenty thousand pounds)] to his daughter [IJ] if she should survive him and attain the age of 25 years and by clause ____ the Testator directed that the residue of his estate (herein and therein called 'the Trust Fund') should be held upon trust for his wife [LJ] absolutely

(C) The said [IJ] having attained the age of 25 years and having accepted no benefit whatsoever from the said legacy or from the Trust Fund is desirous of disclaiming the said pecuniary legacy of [£20,000], to the intent that the said sum shall form part of the Trust Fund and be held upon trust for [LJ] absolutely

NOW THIS DEED WITNESSETH that the said [IJ] HEREBY DISCLAIMS the said pecuniary legacy of [£20,000] given to her by the Will to the intent that the said sum shall form part of the Trust Fund

IN WITNESS etc.

NOTES

1. No election is needed or available for capital tax relief to apply to disclaimers.
2. No stamp duty is payable and no certificate is required.

Discretionary Will Trust Clause

(a) In this clause the following expressions shall have the following meanings:

  (i) 'the Specified date' shall mean the date on which shall expire the period of twenty-three calendar months from the date of my death or such earlier date as my Trustees shall by deed appoint

  (ii) 'the Beneficiaries' shall mean my said wife any issue of mine living at my death or born within twenty-one years after the death of the survivor of me and my said wife and any spouse or dependant of such issue

(*b*) My Trustees shall hold the Trust Fund or any part or parts thereof and the income thereof upon such trusts and with and subject to such powers and provisions if any for the benefit of all or such one or more exclusive of the other or others of the Beneficiaries as my Trustees shall before the Specified date in their absolute discretion appoint

(*c*) Subject thereto until the Specified date my Trustees shall have power in their absolute discretion to pay or apply the whole or any part or parts of the income of the Trust Fund to or for the benefit of all or such one or more exclusive of the other or others of the Beneficiaries and subject thereto shall accumulate the same

(*d*) Subject thereto at the Specified date my Trustees shall hold the Trust Fund and the income thereof upon the trusts of this Will as if this clause had not applied

(*e*) The foregoing powers in this clause shall be exercisable whether or not administration of the Trust Fund shall have been completed and whether or not probate of this my Will shall have been obtained

NOTES

1. It is anticipated that this clause will be inserted after the standard clause creating a trust for sale over residue, which will also direct the payment of debts funeral administration and testamentary expenses, and that the net residue remaining will be defined as 'the Trust Fund'.
2. If a nil rate band legacy is to be given or discretionary trusts, an additional sub-clause is required in (a):

   '(iii) 'the legacy' shall mean the greatest value (if any) which such legacy can have within the nil rate band of inheritance tax applicable at the date of my death which does not cause inheritance tax to be charged (other than at the said nil rate) in respect of my estate (as defined by section 5 of the Inheritance Tax Act 1984) as a consequence of my death'

   and the words 'the legacy' should be substituted for 'the Trust Fund' wherever they appear in the clause.

3. It is anticipated that the expression 'my Trustees' is in the Will defined to include the executors and trustees for the time being and from time to time of the Will.

Appointment pursuant to a Discretionary Will Trust Clause

THIS DEED OF APPOINTMENT is made this .... day of ....

198.....BY [KL] of ....

and [MN] of ....
(hereinafter together called 'the Trustees')

WHEREAS
(A) [OP] (hereinafter called 'the Testator') died on .... having made his last Will (hereinafter called 'the Will') on .... whereby he appointed the Trustees to be the executors and trustees thereof
(B) No grant of Probate of the Will has yet been obtained by the Trustees
(C) By Clause X(*b*) of the Will the Trustees were directed to hold the Trust Fund (as in the Will defined) or any part or parts thereof and the income thereof upon such trusts and with and subject to such powers and provisions if any for the benefit of all or such one or more exclusive of the other or others of the Beneficiaries (as in the Will defined) as the Trustees should before the Specified date in their absolute discretion appoint
(D) The Trustees are desirous of exercising the powers given to them by Clause X of the Will or any other power them enabling in manner hereinafter appearing [and by virtue of clause X(*c*) without first having obtained a grant to the Will or completed administration] in favour of the Testator's wife and issue who are Beneficiaries

NOW THIS DEED WITNESSETH as follows:

1. IN EXERCISE of the powers conferred on them by Clause X of the Will and of all or any other power them enabling the Trustees HEREBY APPOINT that the Trust Fund and the income thereof shall henceforth be held upon the following trusts and with and subject to the following provisions in favour of the wife and issue of the Testator all of whom are Beneficiaries:
   (*a*) as to the property investments and cash specified in the Schedule hereto UPON TRUST for such of the children of the Testator [PP QP and RP] as shall attain the age of thirty years if more than one in equal shares absolutely provided that if any said child shall die before attaining a vested interest leaving issue surviving him or her such issue as shall attain the age of twenty-one years shall

take if more than one in equal shares per stirpes the share which such deceased child would have taken had he or she survived to take a vested interest but so that no issue shall take whose parent is alive and so capable of taking and subject thereto

(*b*) UPON TRUST for [Mrs P] absolutely

2. [Add such administrative powers as are considered necessary, for example, those set out in Precedent A]
3. It is hereby certified that this instrument falls within category F in the Schedule to the Stamp Duty (Exempt Instruments) Regulations 1987.

IN WITNESS etc.

THE SCHEDULE

NOTES

1. As to the effect of this appointment, see Chapter IV. In particular, note that it will not itself be a parent settlement within TA 1988, s 663 (s 437) nor will it be caught by s 683, (s 457) since the settlor, OP, is dead. No stamp duty is payable.
2. The perpetuity period applicable to this appointment is the perpetuity period for the Will itself (lives of living beneficiaries plus 21 years), but here there is no possibility of breach.
3. The power of appointment should be exercised before grant if the surviving spouse is to benefit, to avoid the need to pay inheritance tax on application for the grant and later recover it.

Gift of Life Interest

THIS DEED OF GIFT is made the . . . . day of . . . .

198 . . . . .BETWEEN [ST] of . . . .

(hereinafter called 'the Life Tenant') of the one part and [UV] of . . . .

. . . . and [WX]

of . . . .
(hereinafter together called 'the Trustees') of the other part

WHEREAS

(A) [YT] (hereinafter called 'the Testator') died on . . . . having made his last Will (hereinafter called 'the Will') dated . . . . with one Codicil (hereinafter called 'the Codicil') dated . . . . whereby he appointed the Trustees to be the executors and trustees of the Will and the Codicil

(B) The Trustees obtained a grant of Probate of the Will and the Codicil on . . . . out of the Probate [.................... District] Registry of the Family Division

(C) By Clause X of the Codicil the Testator gave all his shares (hereinafter called 'the Shares') in [Z Ltd] to his Trustees to hold the same to pay the income to the Life Tenant for her life and on her death the Testator directed that the Shares should form part of the Trust Fund (as in the Will defined)

(D) The Life Tenant is desirous of assigning her life interest in the Shares to the Trustees to the intent that the Shares shall form part of the Trust Fund

NOW THIS DEED WITNESSETH as follows:

1. [By way of variation of the dispositions of the Will] the Life Tenant hereby assigns all that her interest under the Codicil in the Shares unto the Trustees to hold the same upon the trusts of the Trust Fund declared in the Will as if the Life Tenant were dead
2. [Election if desired]
3. [Stamp duty certificate]

IN WITNESS etc.

NOTES

1. If an election is desired, insert one as for Precedent A.
2. The gift takes effect as an assignment of the life interest to the reversioner, by way of variation if desired. Note that if the life interest is disclaimed (assuming that it is possible to do so) the disclaimer will automatically be related back to death either under s 142 or, if more than two years has elapsed since the date of death, under s 93 (as to which see page 37) although see page 34 for the problems which could arise on a disclaimer if the initial gift is wrongly worded.
3. If no election is to be made, the deed will take effect as a lifetime gift by the life tenant of the value of the trust fund at the date of the deed. This gift is a potentially exempt transfer for inheritance tax.
4. The Stamp Duty Category is L.

Variation of a Deceased's Joint Tenancy Interest

THIS DEED OF VARIATION is made the .... day of ....

198 ....BETWEEN [AA] of ....

(hereinafter called 'Mr B') of the one part and [CC] of ....

.... and [DD]

of ....

(hereinafter together called 'the Trustees') of the third part

WHEREAS

(A) ZA (hereinafter called 'the Testator') died on the .... day of .... having made his last Will (hereinafter called 'the Will') dated .... the Testator appointed the Trustees as executors and trustees of the Will and the Trustees obtained a Grant of Probate out of the Principal [.................. District] Probate Registry of the Family Division on ....

(B) Immediately before the date of his death the Testator owned a beneficial joint tenancy with Mrs A in the property known as .... (hereinafter called 'the Property') which interest of the Testator formed part of his estate at the date of his death

(C) Mrs A wishes to vary the disposition on death of the said joint tenancy interest of the Testator so that the interest shall accrue to Mr B in place of Mrs A and so that Mrs A and Mr B shall hold the property as beneficial joint tenants

NOW THIS DEED WITNESSETH:

1. The disposition on the death of the Testator of his joint tenancy interest in the property shall be varied so that the said interest shall be treated as passing to Mr B as at the date of the death of the Testator and Mrs A hereby conveys to herself and Mr B all that the freehold interest in the property to hold the same unto Mrs A and Mr B as beneficial joint tenants absolutely
2. Mrs A and Mr B hereby covenant with the Trustees to pay any inheritance tax leviable in respect of the estate of the Testator which would not have been leviable if this deed had not been executed
3. [Election if desired]
4. [Stamp Duty Certificate, category L]

IN WITNESS etc.

Appendix

The rates of inheritance tax depend on the date of the relevant death. The relevant scales are:

TRANSFERS AFTER 17 MARCH 1986

		DEATH SCALE		GROSS			LIFETIME SCALE	
Cumulative chargeable transfers net	*Rate*	*Rate on net fraction*	*Cumulative tax*	*Cumulative chargeable transfers*	*Rate*	*Rate on net fraction*	*Cumulative tax*	*Cumulative chargeable transfers net*
£	%		£	£	%		£	£
0– 71,000	nil	nil	nil	0– 71,000	nil	nil	nil	0– 71,000
71,000– 87,800	30	3/7	7,200	71,000– 95,000	15	3/17	3,600	71,000– 91,400
87,800–109,900	35	7/13	19,100	95,000–129,000	17½	7/33	9,550	91,450–119,400
109,900–130,900	40	2/3	33,100	129,000–164,000	20	1/4	16,550	119,450–147,450
130,900–154,000	45	9/11	52,000	164,000–206,000	22½	9/31	26,000	147,450–180,000
154,000–197,500	50	1	77,500	206,000–257,000	25	1/3	38,750	180,000–218,250
197,500–206,500	55	11/9	110,500	257,000–317,000	27½	11/29	55,250	218,250–261,750
over 206,500	60	3/2	—	over 317,000	30	3/7	—	over 261,750

TRANSFERS AFTER 16 MARCH 1987

	DEATH SCALE			GROSS		LIFETIME SCALE		
Cumulative chargeable transfers net	*Rate*	*Grossing up fraction*	*Cumulative tax*	*Cumulative chargeable transfers*	*Rate*	*Grossing up fraction*	*Cumulative tax*	*Cumulative chargeable transfers net*
£	%		£	£	%		£	£
0– 90,000	nil	nil	nil	0– 90,000	nil	nil	nil	0– 90,000
90,000–125,000	30	3/7	15,000	90,000–140,000	15	3/17	7,500	90,000–132,500
125,000–173,000	40	2/3	47,000	140,000–220,000	20	1/4	23,500	132,500–196,500
173,000–228,000	50	1	102,000	220,000–330,000	25	1/3	51,000	196,500–279,000
over 228,000	60	3/2	—	over 330,000	30	3/7	—	over 279,000

BUDGET PROPOSALS FOR TRANSFERS AFTER 14 MARCH 1988

	DEATH SCALE			GROSS			*LIFETIME SCALE*	
Cumulative chargeable transfers net	*Rate*	*Grossing up fraction*	*Cumulative tax*	*Cumulative chargeable transfers*	*Rate*	*Grossing up fraction*	*Cumulative tax*	*Cumulative chargeable transfers net*
£	%		£	£	%		£	£
0–110,000	nil	nil	nil	0–110,000	nil	nil	nil	0–110,000
over 110,000	40	2/3	—	over 110,000	20	1/4	—	over 110,000